SOLO II

Further Monologues for Drama

John Goodwin and Bill Taylor

Hodder & Stoughton
LONDON SYDNEY AUCKLAND

Preface

Solo II is a second volume of monologues presenting ideas through character. While the first **Solo** book explored themes relevant to the teenage world, this new volume aims to put the teenage experience into context as part of the continuing growing-up process which takes place throughout life. We have introduced a broader range of characters from different age and social groupings (e.g. *Kim, Rico, Henry*) and extended the monologue form to provide greater opportunity for character development and analysis.

Each of the monologues tells a story or presents a viewpoint from which participants can develop ideas through a variety of methods, e.g. drama role play, hot seating, discussion, written work, etc. (The introduction to **Solo** gives more details of ways to explore ideas.) The follow-up section at the back of the book contains suggestions as to how each specific monologue or set can be developed.

Many of the monologues in this volume are interrelated, with two or more characters linked together to provide a broader perspective to an issue or incident. Those monologues bracketed together in the contents list form part of a set. Generally all monologues can also be used individually.

By extending the format of the first volume, it is hoped that **Solo II** will prove useful both within schools and as a starting-point to workshop drama for youth and community theatre groups.

John Goodwin and Bill Taylor

Contents

5   Viewpoints

6   Problems

see also Secrets and Gina sections

7   Gina

8   Follow-up Work

1
Lifestyles

Lisa

(Lisa is in her last year at school and has just changed her image.)

I got really fed up, 'Lisa', I said to myself 'You're the same as everybody else, boring, really really boring and then I thought . . . you're going to do something about this . . . something different . . . about a week later in the precinct I saw this punk . . . you know . . . mohican, leather, chains . . . the lot, and I thought that's for me . . . everybody was looking at him as he sat there . . . he didn't do anything . . . not shouting, swearing or jumping about . . . but he was different . . . one little kid stood and stared for hours . . . so . . . I did it . . . there and then . . . I walked straight into a hairdressers and said 'I want a Mohican'.

When she started shaving it off . . . all down one side of my head . . . I thought . . ., what have I done? . . . but it was too late. When she'd finished I looked up in the mirror. As I walked out of the shop I knew I was different . . . special.

I expected my Mum and Dad to go wild . . . throw me out of the house and all that . . . what did they say? . . . 'That's nice dear' and carried on looking at the telly. There was some fuss at school not quite a holocaust but a few funny looks. Next thing I know somebody else in our year has the same done to her. Soon it'll be the whole of the school. What have you got to do to be different?

Charlotte

(Charlotte is sixteen and has recently become a vegetarian. She decided to do this because of her feelings about the cruelty involved in killing animals for food.)

It happened back in the summer. We had these friends to stay with us and they didn't eat meat. My Mum didn't know that and cooked the usual Sunday dinner to greet their arrival: roast beef, baked potatoes, Yorkshire Pudding and all the trimmings. "Sorry", they say, "we don't eat meat." Mum was so put out and all her food plans for the weekend were ruined.

She sulked all weekend but I seemed to get on with them really well. We started talking . . . cruelty in breeding animals just to feed humans . . . it really makes you think. I thought food without meat would be boring, but the kind of food they eat – savory flans, nut roast, vegetable curry, leeks in white sauce – it all seemed really exciting.

So after they'd gone I said 'That's it, I'm not going to eat any more meat'. Mum gave me one of those looks which meant 'another one of her fads', but I was determined. 'I'm going to do it' I said 'you just see'. That was six months ago and I've not eaten any meat since. What's more the whole family are now vegetarians. My brother was the last to be converted. He'd tuck into his bacon and sausage as usual whilst we had cheese flan. Then I'd sit very close to him and whisper in his ear: 'Enjoy your dead flesh . . . your pig's brains, bones and skin.' At last it got to him and turning green he pushed his plate away pretending he was full as he tried not to puke up.

The worst time is when we go out for a meal. Like to Gran's. I don't think she can quite understand and will insist on giving us plates full of meat. When we look confused and unsure of our next move she'll say: 'Eat it up, it's only tongue, it'll not harm you.' The very thought . . . eating the tongue of a dead cow. Revolting! Fish is just as bad. Imagine a clear mountain stream: a young fish swimming freely and happily. The next moment, a hook sunk into its throat and just for human greed; or young calves butchered in a slaughter house; or the horror of battery hens, kept in stinking sheds, never allowed to see the light of day.

So next time you sit down to a plate full of dead flesh, pig's brains, bones and skin thinly disguised as a pork pie, remember, there is an alternative. And it doesn't mean boring food or not eating. Vegetarian meals are different, why not give them a try?

Kieron

(Kieron is on holiday with his parents.)

We were sitting on a beach on a typical cold British summer's day. Shivering and bored I wondered why I had agreed to come on holiday with 'the parents'. It looked like rain any minute and the last thing I fancied was the thought of a swim. I mean in the middle of May, I ask you?

Yet quite close by is this old boy doing the back stroke out there in the fridge-like sea. He must have been sixty at least. He wasn't in for long and hobbled up the pebble shore. With his green bathers and dead-white body he looked like a moving piece of celery that you get off the market: kind of limp looking. He made his way to a dog, a bundle of clothes, pats the dog, shivers and heads once more for the grey water. He's in a couple of minutes on his back and kicking his feet in the air.

Then it's out again and back to the dog. All these comings and goings are making me dizzy just watching. He rubs himself down with his towel, pats the dog and settles down to rest for a bit. As he sits there, the tide is coming in very sharp and the waves are really close to his gear. Yet he doesn't seem to notice and just pats his dog. Then I sussed it. He's blind. I could just see the dog harness, red reflectors and all. A family next to him finally shout about the nearness of the waves and he feels for his gear and moves it back up the beach. For the next half an hour I watch, transfixed. Finally he got up and off he went along the top of the sea wall and out of sight.

I don't know if he was local or if somebody brought him in a car. But one thing is sure; that sixty year old blind man put me to shame. So I thought I'd better make an effort, perhaps the sea wasn't that cold after all. I got as far as taking my shoes and socks off, but my toes curled and went a funny blue colour. I thought better of it. That old bloke must have been some hero.

Kim

(Kim is a disabled girl and confined to a wheelchair.)

There's no need to feel sorry for me. I can manage perfectly well. So long as people don't fuss and try to do everything for me. I've got used to the staring, the whispers. I just don't even notice, as long as people don't fuss.

It's the Christmas party at school tonight and I've already had a row about it. 'Do you think you ought to go love . . . it might be difficult for you . . . you don't want any accidents?' That's my mother, one of life's worriers. But Dad knew I had made up my mind and that was that. So I won't be able to join in the dancing, so what? There's plenty of our class who have no intention of making a fool of themselves. I just want to be there, with everybody else.

I've got a new dress 'specially and Samina will be coming round to call any minute. Samina's a special friend. She's the only Asian girl in our class and she had a row with her parents about going tonight. They're dead strict about her going anywhere. But she'll be here anytime now if I know Samina.

I've looked forward to this party tonight for ages. Dad

bought a special easy car to put my wheelchair in and just before we go out I say the order of exactly what I have to do: car door open, position chair, brake on wheelchair, move side of chair down, arms behind, hands on car seat, lean backwards, weight on hands, move body, lift legs into car, right, left, Dad folds the chair and places it in the boot of the car and off we go. As simple as that.

Samina and me have done a few things together. Because of her religion and that she can't go swimming at school. She always has to wear trousers. So whilst the rest of the class go off swimming we have a table tennis room to ourselves. It's a great laugh.

She said she'd be here twenty minutes ago. Still I expect the party will have only just started. I'm sure she'll be here soon, sure of it.

Katie

(Katie has followed the rise of a particular pop group and has just heard that the group is going to disband.)

I just couldn't believe it. I was gob smacked. I've followed that group for two years. I saw them at a concert before they ever really became famous. They were a support group then and I went to the stage door to get their autographs. There was just me and a couple of lads; they talked to us cracked a few jokes and even asked me what my name was. That programme is on my bedroom wall, next to posters, photos and the album sleeve. I watched them become famous, song in the charts, national tour topping the bill, TV interviews, the lot. Then this.

They weren't the same as any ordinary group. You wouldn't call them a pop group. They had something to say, not just a loud sound. Peace was what they stood for and they gave all their money away to charity and lived off £200 a week. Not many groups would do that. I've written to them every week for ages and always had a letter back within a few days. The last one said: 'As you may have heard the group are splitting up from June this year, with all members expecting to move on and progress when that time arrives.' They even made a joke about it and are printing new sweat shirts with: 'Banana Split', 'Trouser Split', 'Split Peas', 'The Splits', and their name on, with the date they split up.

I won't buy one. I couldn't bring myself to do it. I shall have to change my image now. After all, they are a thing of the past.

Credita

(The year is AD2100. People live in domed cities, protected from Earth's contaminated atmosphere. Citizens can achieve great wealth and status if they work hard. Those who do not achieve can only afford to get by on handouts given by generous citizens. However, the Cities' philosophy is 'Look After Yourself' and anyone caught giving charity could be fined or exiled by the authorities. In this self-sufficient world, helping others is seen as an attempt to stop them looking after themselves.

Credita is a young woman, awaiting her appearance before the City Judge.)

I used to see her each night on Strata Four, an old withered woman with her hand outstretched, waiting for a few dollars for a glass of Nourish or a loaf of Vitameal. Of course, I never stopped. As my father used to say, 'If you were poor, would you allow someone to help you?'. I knew I wouldn't. No matter how bad things were, I'd always want to protect my right to look after myself. Pride can only help you if you believe in it.

And yet it seemed strange that the woman begged. I mean, I understood the problem. Her pride had left her. And I knew that giving her dollars would prevent her pride from returning. And yet, she seemed so old and fragile. Surely her death-day was not far away and when that arrived her pride would be gone completely. So I gave her a hundred-dollar piece. I know it was wrong, but I couldn't help myself. It was only a hundred dollars after all. Less than I give the young children who come up to me and ask if I'd like to be told the time.

I didn't know the guard was watching. But I felt her hand on my shoulder as I gave the woman the hundred-dollar piece. The old woman called out 'Half past eight' and pretended she was selling me the time. But the guard could tell she had no watch and no licence to sell the time. So that was that. The guard brought me here to await the City Judge.

I'm afraid of what will happen. No defence is permitted for charity. And what could I say anyway? That I felt sorry for her. No, charity is bad enough, if I were tried for pity or arrogance as well it would mean certain exile. No one can survive in the outside.

As for the old woman, I suppose she is still there,

clutching her hundred-dollar piece. It seems so stupid. If begging is not a crime, why is charity?

Emma

(Emma is seventeen and has just persuaded her parents to let her have her first teenage party at home.)

The first thing is don't call it a party. If you do parents always fear the worst: drugs, sex, booze and trouble. No, call it a 'little get together' of friends and you might get away with it. At least that's what my mates said. So I tried it.

'You mean . . . a party?', said Mum. My tactics shot to the winds, I stumbled: 'Well . . . I er . . . that is . . .'

But most unexpectedly Dad, like a true knight in shining armour, came to my rescue: 'Well I don't see why not, so long as it's not too many and you don't make too much noise'. But Mum was more perceptive: 'I think Emma would want us to go out for the evening of the party, isn't that right Emma?' Dad was more predictable: 'Us go out. Why?'

After conditions of time, number of invitations, booze restrictions and miscellaneous behaviour clauses the deal was done.

They left at seven, the first of the gang arrived at half past and despite a few wobbly moments it was a great success. Quite the highlight of the social calendar was the general opinion of our par . . . whooops . . . 'get together'. No broken bottles, no vomiting on the carpet not even an orgy or a punch thrown. The wobbles came in the form of a china duck being beheaded, a snooker ball nicked, a neighbour's complaints and a potential major wobble of a car full of unexpected guests of the 'unsavoury' and 'uninvited' variety. But a tube of super glue, a shorter game of snooker, a grovel to the neighbours and the firm denial of the location of a party and the threat of the imminent return of my parents saved the day.

Mum and Dad returned at half past eleven. The guests had left at twenty-eight minutes past. It was timed to perfection. I gave them both a glass of sherry and you could see the amazement on their faces. They didn't even find the tube of super glue.

I have to thank them that's for sure. You see I wanted to prove to them that I could do it. You know, trust and all that. Besides I wouldn't mind a 'little get together' next month and the behaviour clauses had to be met for that to happen.

Beryl

Beryl is sixty-five. Here she recalls her experiences as a farm worker during the war.)

I remember the day I first met Mr Tomlinson. 'You better be worth it, lass', he said. He hadn't wanted women working on his farm, but most of his labourers had been called up and after a year of trying to manage almost single-handed he'd decided to 'take the risk', as he saw it. I'd been working for a few months as a welder. It'd been a good time. Most of my friends were at the factory. The hours had been long – ten-hour days sometimes – but there was great sense of, well, achievement I suppose. Silly to think that it took a world war to prove that women could work as well as men. Then my brother was killed in action. I was eighteen. My parents persuaded me to volunteer for the Women's Land Army. They were afraid that if I stayed in the city I'd be a victim of bombing raids. Losing Norman made them very cautious and protective of their only remaining child.

I didn't want to go, but for their sake I enrolled. Meeting Mr Tomlinson didn't exactly help matters. He was a harsh, grumpy man. We worked for ten, twelve, sometimes fourteen hours a day – ploughing, digging drains, milking the cows – and in return I got my bed and board and what amounted to little more than 'pocket money'. There were two recruits on the farm – me and Sandra. We got on well together. Had to. We shared a double bed in the draughty loft of the farmhouse. Sandra was great fun. Very big and strong with a laugh that could drown a fog horn. She'd been a domestic cook before the war and used to refer to Mrs Tomlinson's cooking as 'Hitler's secret weapon'. In a way I envied Sandra. Mr Tomlinson let her drive the tractor while I nearly always got lumbered with the cows.

Then one day Sandra agreed to show me how to use the tractor. We didn't tell Tomlinson of course. We were out in the field ploughing and planting. I was amazed how simple driving a tractor was. You just needed to be positive. The controls were heavy to work. For the rest of the day Sandra and I took turns. We had a great time. When we got back to the farm, Tomlinson was in a state of frustrated rage. I don't know what annoyed him more – me driving the tractor, or the fact that I'd done a good job of it. In all my time at the farm he only once found something nice to say to me. He told me I had a 'shapely pair of legs'. And he was drunk when he said it.

▽ Dan

(Dan is the landlord of 'The Plough'.)

It seemed like a good idea. Trade was a bit quiet, so I thought why not? We'd had a darts championship last year and that pulled in a good crowd. Pool seemed a natural choice. There's some really good players that come in here. The pool room is packed most nights. I put in two fruit machines and it's turned into a good little money spinner, and in a village pub you need all the trade you can get. It's young lads really, but I don't allow no leathers and there's no trouble.

We had thirty entries for the competition, all drawn out on paper. There was an entry fee, with proceeds going to charity. All the locals entered and I arranged sandwiches for the competition nights, right through to the finals. When Phyllis Arrowsmith entered I was surprised – she didn't seem the type. An old lady, living a quiet life, she never came in the pub. But there was her name on the sheet. At first we all thought it was a joke. But up she turns for the match and even brings her own cue. Faces were a picture to watch that night I can tell you. For a start she pockets a ball straight from the break and wins the game inside five minutes. The lad she was playing choked on his lager and you can guess what his mates called him.

But soon it was his turn to laugh. She beat the lot that night. The pub went very quiet as one by one she outplayed them all. The room was packed, folks crowded round the door and along the passage. She packed up her cue, shook hands with the lads and headed for the door with a place on final's night in her pocket. Everybody just stood there and watched her go. As she got to the door a voice shouted out: 'Come on love, I'll buy you a drink. I reckon you deserve it.' She stopped and turned slowly. 'It's very kind of you to offer', she said 'but I feel quite tired'. 'Just a quick drink, go on spoil yourself.' A smile came on her face and that was the beginning of one of the best nights we've had in here. She didn't drink a lot, but talk about laugh. She said she was drunk on the atmosphere.

And next week its final's night. I've applied for an extension, phoned the local paper and ordered plenty of extra drink. The word's round, a local star is made and will appear next week at 'The Plough'.

▽ Phyllis

I've watched snooker on the television for ages. It's one of my favourite programmes. You really feel as though you're there with them. The cloth of the table looks so green and the colours of the balls seem to shine out. It all goes very quiet, all still as they concentrate so hard. And the shots they play, it takes your breath away. I could watch it over and over again.

So when they organised this pool competition in the village it seemed only natural to enter. When my husband died two years ago, his snooker table was still standing in our back room. I covered it over and the dust gathered over it. I'd never played when he was alive. He said it wasn't a game for women and I didn't argue. But I'd watched him play, him and his friends. Pool, snooker, billiards.

It was after the last championship on the television, I thought right come on Phyllis you can have a go at this my girl. So I took the covers off the table, neatly folded them away and put a few balls on the table. I'd seen them chalk the cue so I knew what to do. I placed the white near a red, bent down, placed the cue over my fingers, drew back the cue and pushed it forward as hard as I could. I missed the ball completely and twisted my back. But I wasn't going to let it get the best of me.

I must have played on that table for hours. It was a wet afternoon in March I remember. I knocked balls right off the table, the clock off the mantlepiece, tripped over the cat, but I didn't give up.

Next day I was stiff as a board and had pains in my neck. 'Phyllis' I said to myself, 'you're being daft, playing these kinds of tricks at your age'. So I covered over the table again and left it at that. Went back to television, and reading the newspaper.

2
Our World

Rico

(Rico is thirteen. Like thousands of other children, he lives on the streets of Mexico City. His mother is dead and his father has fled across the border to America in search of a better life. Rico survives as best he can.)

When the traffic is busy, I go along the line of cars with my rag. For a few cents I wash windscreens. When I have some money I maybe buy some chewing gum to sell. I have done this for one year now. Sometimes I miss my family and wish that we were still together. Most I miss my mother. I see my sister sometimes. She also lives on the streets but she is older and has a different life. So I stay with my friends. We sleep on the roof of one of the factories in the north of the city. When it is cold there is the steam from the machines to keep us warm. But during the day it is best to be alone. Sometimes the police come and take us. Sometimes we are beaten and locked away. But sometimes they don't bother. I walk and ask for money, but I am not crippled so it is harder for me to get money this way. Sometimes I take things that are not mine. I always need something to sell, so that I can buy gum and cigarettes to make more money. There are five in my group. The youngest is seven. We must all eat.

One day I think my father will come back for me. In America we can have dollars and have a place to live and do well. I tried to go to America but I was caught and sent back. One day I will get there. This is what I think at night, when I sleep.

Michael

(Michael Dunstable is a journalist working in East Africa. This is a report he sent back.)

Each morning the dead are carried out of the village, shrouded in sackcloth. These tight bundles were once bodies, their bones meticulously picked clean. The bundles are laid out in a line on the dust. The names of the dead are taken. Catalogued and forgotten. Indifferent formalities. Afterwards the stick heaps are taken up again and returned to the village. Laid to rest. Disposed of.

Mothers mourn their babies. Men their wives. Children their parents. In this cramped settlement are ten thousand starving souls, living on top of each other but each alone and separate in their grief. We feel we ought to help. We talk about millions. But it is too little too late. Hysterical sympathy prolongs the suffering. The best we can offer these people is oblivion.

Last night I slept for the first time since I arrived here. I dreamt. A vivid nightmare. I was tearing the last pieces of flesh from the limbs of a young child. Gorging myself on thin strands of sinew. I ate without appetite as the child watched me. Silently. His hand reached out for a small piece of his own flesh. I ignored him quite automatically and continued to feed myself. I gave him a dollar. He stuffed it into his mouth. He choked.

When I woke this morning thirteen more villagers were dead. Thirteen more bundles of sackcloth. Thirteen. Lucky for some.

▽ Grant

(Grant has just begun a career as a customs officer.)

I just saw the case, it was as simple as that. I stared hard at the brown mock leather. It was identical to the one we had used in the training session, almost the exact colour, size and style. And now it was there before my eyes, the real thing. This happened shortly before I was due to take a lunch break and if it had been five minutes later I would have missed the whole incident.

After the case I noticed the hand carrying it and then a black face, very nervous looking and shifting eyes. The eyes were searching, seeking out the details of the surroundings. I took a deep breath and asked very clearly and slowly the usual 'Anything to declare, sir?'. He didn't answer. I repeated the same question and still the black face did not respond, no lips moved. I reached for the case and he took a step back. I moved my hand closer to the case and the black arm offered it up.

As I looked then, the case in my hands, I knew. There could be no doubt. All that training. I knew. The bottom would have a false compartment. All the time the black face watched with hard eyes. In seconds my slightly trembling fingers had confirmed the deception, a senior officer was on the scene, the drugs discovered and the man led away.

I didn't see him again. Nobody has told me exactly what has happened yet. I suppose I may have to give evidence in court, no doubt the senior officer will interview me soon. All I know is that I have caught my first drug carrier in my first week at work. What luck! And now as I rerun the whole incident, like a rehearsal for the court, I tell myself that black face was guilty. As guilty as hell and he deserves all the punishment that justice will give him.

▽ Tom

(Tom spends one or two evenings a week as a volunteer prison visitor.)

He just looked at me and asked 'Have you come to make me free?'. 'No', I explained, 'I'm a prison visitor, I've come to talk to you'. He looked away and not a word was said. He sat in silence until the end of the allotted time.

That first meeting with Simeon was five months ago and during those months I have got to know him very well. He's innocent, of that I'm very sure. It's not only the facts of his case but a gut reaction I've got whenever I think about him.

The details of his case began to emerge slowly and in fragments. For several sessions he would sit in silence, just as at our first meeting. I'd visited others who had not wanted to talk and the silence didn't worry me, I was prepared to wait. One day I asked 'Would you like me to read you something?'. 'Shakespeare,' he said 'would you read me some of that?'. Now that wasn't quite what I'd expected, but if he wanted Shakespeare, well who was I to argue.

We started with *Othello* and his understanding was amazing, his knowledge of the English language incredible. Yet he could not understand why Othello was obsessed with his wife's jealousy, why didn't he take another wife or two wives, he asked. When I explained that it was our custom for a man to have only one wife he was utterly confused.

Simeon comes from a small village near Nairobi in Kenya and was taught to read and write by a missionary teacher. He was, I understand, a 'star' pupil. With his knowledge of English he was able to get a job in one of the game reserves as a tourist guide. A group of Canadians became regular visitors to the reserve and befriended Simeon. They told of wonderful opportunities in their country and how it might be possible for him to visit them there. The arrangements were made, Simeon was to go to Canada on a six months' special agricultural work scheme and return to Kenya and teach those in his village all he had learnt. His friends even arranged for his suitcases for the journey and these arrived the day before he was due to fly out to Ontario.

His flight touched down in London, where he was due to meet his friends and then travel on with them to Canada. He had to go through customs, his luggage was searched, drugs found in the cases and his journey ended in a prison in England. His friends never appeared and he did not know their addresses. His prison sentence is due to end next month and I understand he will be flown back to Nairobi, immediately rearrested, but put back into prison and his family sued by the British government for the expense of his stay in a British jail.

Usually I don't get involved with my prison clients. After all, I'm not there to pass judgments and all information is of course strictly confidential. It's best to keep detached from it all. But with Simeon, that has not been possible. I am convinced that he has done absolutely nothing wrong and yet he has lost everything.

▽ Simeon

(Simeon comes from a small tribal village near Nairobi in Kenya.)

I cannot sleep at nights. The time passes so slowly as I lie half awake, half asleep, and at these times I see faces in my mind. Always the same faces. There is my family at home and above them the red skies, so red. Then the white faces, many white faces. Sometimes the white faces talk, only I cannot hear their words. I try very hard and strain my ears till they ache but I cannot tell what they say.

I do not know what will happen to me. Why did my white friends not come to meet me? There is some terrible mistake and I am caught up in it all and there is nobody here that I can talk to. Nobody to listen, to find the white friends from Canada.

I pray to God that he will deliver me up, out of the belly of this whale and like Jonah truth and righteousness will find its path. God knows I am innocent of everything and that I have done no wrong.

Mrs Edwards was a fine lady who taught me to read and write and to love Jesus. 'There is no place in our hearts for hate and bad thoughts, Jesus loved his enemies even as they did him to death', she would say to us all and we would repeat it after her. I wish Mrs Edwards was here now, she would believe me. As I lie in this cold British jail my heart is filled with so many bad thoughts for the white faces. I only wish to be with my family and back in my home.

3
Secrets

▽ Cathy

(Cathy Wilson is a teacher in a comprehensive school.)

Donna Richards is missing. She has been missing for three days. The police have been informed. They issued a description. 'Donna is of average height, with straight dark hair. She has a small scar on her forehead. She was last seen wearing black shoes, jeans and a brown coat.'

An average description you might say for an average sort of girl. But I know Donna, she is a pupil in the school where I teach and I would say she certainly isn't average, whatever that may mean.

She was in the first year when I first taught her. She would sit in a corner, never speak, never smile. Then one day we were writing animal poems and she wrote this amazing poem about a dolphin. It was really outstanding and clearly all her own work. As the class were leaving at the end of the lesson I asked her to stay behind for a brief chat. She was quiet then, reluctant to stay, but over the next few weeks she became more trusting and ready to open up a conversation. She would talk to me, but in class was as quiet and withdrawn as usual. She started to write, at home, in class, every spare moment she had. It poured out of her, poems, stories and a very much longer piece of writing. One poem was so good that I sent it off to a literary competition.

Then only last week Donna went back to her silence. She sat in the back corner of the classroom and wouldn't speak to me or anyone. I was worried but she shunned any form of contact.

On Wednesday we had arranged to visit the local newspaper offices as part of our work in English and Donna had been particularly interested in the visit. Donna didn't make the trip. So, she could have been ill, perhaps flu or something. But somehow I was worried. I knew she had a pretty unhappy life out of school and she had mentioned that she lived with her Dad. I found the address from the school records. 101 Maple Drive. Should I go round? There was no record of a phone number. You're being silly I told myself, but something inside me made me climb into my car and set off for Maple Drive.

As I stood there on the front doorstep I felt really uncomfortable, prying into Donna's private life and with only one day of absence from school. The door opened, I explained who I was and why I had come. I expected to be told that Donna was fine and that would be the end of it. But Donna's father frowned.

'She told me about that trip. I gave her £5 especially.'

There was an awkward silence. Her disappearance was reported to the police. It seemed the only sensible thing to do. That was three days ago and Donna is still missing.

▽ # Rosemary

(Rosemary Simpson is the manageress of a local super-market.)

Yes, I recognise the girl in the photograph. It's Donna Richards. She's worked here for about two months now on a part-time basis shelf-stacking, two hours in the week and all day Saturday. She told me she was fifteen. I didn't check. I didn't know she was lying. How do you mean I could be prosecuted for underage employment? She certainly looked fifteen and I'm too busy to go checking birth certificates or anything like that. I've got a busy supermarket to run and we're short staffed as it is.

No, I didn't know she was missing. She was a good worker, though she failed to turn up to shifts once or twice. When she did come, she kept herself to herself and got on with her work. Not like some of the teenagers we've had here, I can tell you.

I couldn't really say much else about her, she was a part-time shelf filler that's all.

▽ # Mike

(Mike is seventeen and has been friendly with Donna for some time.)

'Donna Richards? Yes I know her, we used to go to school together. Me go out with her? Well that was

some time ago, months at least. I haven'
for some time. Did I know she was mis.
didn't know. Mind you, that Dad of hers tr.
so bad I'm not surprised she's run off. How d.
know she'd run off? Well stands to reason doesn't it,
any fool can see that. Do I know where she might have
gone? No idea. No, she doesn't have any friends. Have
you tried her mother's? Well, if she's not there I don't
have a clue. Shouldn't I be worried for her safety. Yes,
of course.'

That's what I told the police. Only they're not daft,
they'll be back. Maybe pull me into the station 'for ques-
tioning' after all I have got a criminal record. But by then
she should be back. She's alright, not dead or anything
like that. Just needs time to sort a few things out. I really
can't tell you where she is. Don't worry, Donna can look
after herself.

Tim

*(Tim is in the sixth form and is waiting to see his Head of
Year.)*

Let me get it absolutely right . . . word perfect . . . 'I
don't know what made me do it. I've never stolen before.
I know we've never had a lot of cash but we've managed.'
Good so far, now for the incident itself . . . 'It was just
seeing that wallet lying there almost as if it winked at
me. Then Williams whines "Sir someone has stolen my
wallet".

"Where did you leave it boy?" "Changing rooms sir."
"Silly place to leave a wallet." "Yes sir." "How much was
in it?" "Ten pounds sir."

No . . . better make that a fiver . . . that could be
crucial.

Before I knew it I'd said "It was me sir, I stole it".
Everyone turned, amazed. "Come on, Tim, this is not the
time for jokes, Williams has lost five pounds." "I stole the
money sir."

Silence. You could see his mind ticking over. He
changed his tone. "Tim, just come outside a minute.
I'd like a word with you." He still couldn't believe it,
me, Tim Rogers, his star pupil who could never do any
wrong.

Yes that should do, a convincing account . . . just
remember the facial expressions . . . stare at the floor . . .
yes that should really do the trick, that story is bound to
convince anybody.

Lucy

(Lucy is fifteen and has just moved house.)

Do you believe in ghosts? Do you think it is possible
for the dead to come back as spirits and haunt us? Or
is it just our minds playing tricks at times of mental
stress?

I like those words: 'at times of mental stress'. I read
them out of a book. That's what my family think I'm
doing – imagining it all – but I'm not. It really is
happening.

It began when we moved to this cottage. It was to be our dream home. I'd have been happy to stay exactly where we were, but no we had to move to this spooky old place. They told us it was at least two hundred and fifty years old and I can believe it, every lousy year of it.

I was alone. They'd all gone out and it was just getting dark. But a warm night, definitely warm. I felt a cold chill go right through me, like somebody had opened all the doors and windows. I went to check them. All shut tight. Then . . . a presence, difficult to explain, but as if somebody was in the room with me. Not scary, I never felt the spirit – call it what you like – would ever do me any harm.

About the same time I had this dream. Over and over again, always the same, a face, a young girl's face, and the sound of crying. I'm sure it was her crying. There is something about the face, I'm sure she must have lived a long time ago, here in this house. It seems right to me.

Then last week I was alone again. About the same time, the lights began to flicker and there were really weird sounds, then all the lights went out. I was just about to scream, when I saw a faint glow, a lighted candle from the end of the room. It was the girl and she just walked through the wall. I know it sounds stupid, but through a solid wall.

I was crazy enough to tell the rest of the family all about it. Now they won't leave me here on my own. Even said I'd better go and see the doctor. What really bothers me is that she won't come back. I'm sure that she will only visit when I'm here alone. And I want to see her again. I need to know more. But right now it doesn't look as though I'll get a chance.

Kerrie

(Kerrie is fourteen, a rather quiet girl, well liked by friends and acquaintances.)

I once did something really terrible.

I was six years old. My mum had sent me down to the corner shop to get some tea. It was one of those little shops with a bell over the door; you have to wait for the shopkeeper to come out from the back. And I was waiting and waiting. And in front of me on the counter were all kinds of sweets. Gobstoppers and bubbly and chocolate, all there on the counter just waiting to be picked up and taken away. And I knew I could just take what I wanted and no one would know. If the shopkeeper hadn't been out the back watching telly or whatever she was doing it would never have happened. But she didn't come out and I kept waiting and staring until there seemed to be no alternative. I grabbed a packet of winegums and ran out.

I knew it was wrong. I knew it was wrong to get away with it. And I had to go back to the shop again to get the tea and I knew the shopkeeper was looking at me and thinking what a thief I was. I should've owned up. I should've told her about the winegums and paid for them. I had the money. But I didn't. I left the shop with a half pound of tea, and the packet of sweets still hidden in my coat pocket.

I never ate the sweets. I threw them away before I got home. I don't know why I did that. I don't know why I did any of it. Perhaps that's the most terrible thing: I still don't know why.

Hannah

(Hannah is a young woman who lives alone in the centre of a large city.)

I recognised the face instantly, even though I'd only seen him for a few moments. I still can't believe it. I suppose I've been lucky. A narrow escape. But I don't feel lucky. I feel shocked, frightened. I keep thinking 'what if . . .'.

I'd only just got home from work. I put a record on and started to get dinner ready. Then the doorbell rang. And when I answered it, there he was. A small man, but quite stocky, with untidy brown hair and small scrunched-up eyes. He asked me if this was where 'Johnnie' lived. His voice was soft, very polite. I thought he might have been a student, or maybe a community worker or something like that. He certainly wasn't frightening. It'd been raining and he was still quite wet. I mean, if he'd said he was a friend of a friend I'd probably have invited him in for a cup of tea. I know I would have. But I'd had a long day at the shop and I wasn't in a particularly friendly mood. I said 'No, he doesn't live here', in a deliberately impatient tone. He looked very apologetic and hurt. When he'd gone I felt bad about being so rude – he'd probably been trying to find his friend all afternoon.

That was nearly a month ago. And today in the paper, the same face. And the headline – 'Rapist Charged'. A young schoolgirl had been attacked in her home when her parents were out. Apparently the man had pretended to be a friend of her father's. She invited him in. It happened at about eight in the evening. Only a short while after he'd been at my place.

I could have been his victim. Or if only I'd realised the danger I could have prevented him from . . . But at the time, well, it's not something you expect to happen.

First thing tomorrow I'm going to have a chain put on the front door. From now on, I won't give anyone the benefit of the doubt.

▽ Sonia

(Sonia is fourteen.)

I don't know what I was looking for. Mum and Dad had gone out and I decided to go through Dad's bureau. Maybe it was just curiosity. He's always sitting there writing things and I wanted to know what papers and documents he had locked away in there. But I knew it was wrong to snoop like that. I must have known there was something secret hidden away, deep down I must have sensed it.

I knew where he kept the key to the centre drawer that he always keeps locked. Inside there were lots of old forms and papers – Gran's marriage certificate, Dad's will (which I couldn't make head or tail of), old school reports dating back to the war. And then I found it. My birth certificate. The thing I'd been searching for without knowing it.

I'd often wondered why my parents were so much older than my friends' parents. I worked out that mum must've been forty-three when I was born. I mean, they'd got married when they were in their twenties. Seemed a long time to wait. But I never imagined that they weren't actually my parents.

Now I know the truth. The certificate says the name of the mother is someone called Isabel Jordan. The father is 'unknown'. What does that mean? That I have no father?

It hasn't really sunk in yet. I'm an adopted child. Why wasn't I told? The people I've loved and who've cared for me all these years aren't my Mum and Dad at all. Why didn't they tell me?

They'll be getting back soon. Maybe I should put the certificate back in the drawer and not mention it. But I mean, how can I forget? How can I pretend now that I know the truth?

▽ Isabel

(Isabel is thirty, works as a sales manager and is married with a two year old son.)

I was sixteen when she was born, still at school and hoping to stay on into the sixth form. It's not that I didn't want her but I knew I was too young, and there was too much to look forward to. Yes, sometimes I think back and wonder if I was just being selfish. But what could I have offered her then? Her father wouldn't have been much help. He was a courier I'd met on holiday in Spain. We used to see each other each evening while my parents were having dinner or resting in their room. Just a holiday romance. No, not even that. An adventure. He was the first man I ever slept with.

Even if my parents had wanted me to keep the baby I don't think I would have. I wanted to have an abortion at first, but then I remembered an article I'd read about childless couples and how few babies there were for adoption. It seemed the perfect answer. And I think in a way I felt very guilty about what had happened. My parents were horrified to discover their only daughter had got pregnant: it was the kind of thing that only happened to other people. If I carried the child and gave it the chance of a good home with loving parents, I'd be able to turn a mistake into something positive.

Being pregnant was an awful experience. I went away to stay with my aunt. No one was to know my situation, my parents insisted on that. Auntie Cass was very understanding, but I couldn't help wishing I'd stayed among family and friends. Six months is a long time to wait for something to happen. I continued studying, the time passed, the baby was born.

That was all a long time ago now. I tend not to think about it. Life went on. I worked hard to develop my career. I married Jeff. Then a couple of years ago Jamie was born. I enjoy my life. I'm very happy. Things have turned out more or less as I'd hoped.

I think that's why I don't mention the baby. I do wonder what she's like and how she's getting on. But it seems best to forget. No good can come of seeing her now, for either of us.

Henry

(Henry is a business man, with a wife and two teenage children.)

Every morning I kiss Leonie goodbye and take the 7.53 into the city. Same routine every day for the past nineteen years. With one small difference. Five months ago I lost my job.

'We're going to have to let you go', Jackson put it. 'Three months salary in lieu of notice. You'll keep the car of course.' And that was that. Twelve years managing the regional sales team, gone with a shake of the hand. They're making room for new blood. Younger guys with energy and vision. It seems that nobody wants to buy experience any more.

So each morning I arrive in the city, have cup of coffee in the station cafe and start the daily grind of finding a new job. I work in the library most of the time. First, the daily papers. I answer all advertisements for sales or marketing managers. I've even considered assistant manager positions. But so far no luck. Had the occasional interview. The same familiar story – the fast talkers and younger whizzkids get all the jobs. I've been on the circuit, got to know quite a few people. Decent folk most of them. 'Look Henry', they say, 'we'll keep an eye open, let you know if anything falls our way'. So far, nothing.

I can't pretend I'm not getting worried. Leonie doesn't know I lost my job. Couldn't bring myself to tell her. I hoped that a new post would come up and I could tell her I was taking on a fresh challenge. Trouble is, the money's running out. In a few weeks time the bank manager will be wanting to discuss the overdraft. There's still five years left on the mortgage. And Richard and Hilary – they always seem to need money for one thing or another. How could I tell my family I was out of work. Redundant, as they say. Surplus to requirements.

Some nights I sit on the train home, wondering what I'll say when Leonie asks about my day at work. There are moments when I just feel like telling her straight. Share the problem with someone. But that's unthinkable. There must be a way out of this.

4
Relationships

▽ Paul

(Paul is seventeen. He is unemployed. He lives with his disabled mother.)

I don't think much about the future. Don't see much point. My mum says I'm too easily pleased. Lack ambition. I suppose it's true. Give me a guitar and a tune to play and I'm happy. I do my own thing. There's not much money of course. The attendance allowance and widow's pension. I do a bit of busking. Odd jobs. We get by.

Things are gonna be harder now of course. Steve's going away to college in September. I mean, he'll still be around at Christmas and that, but it's gonna be pretty lonely. Just me and my mum.

I met Steve when we were fifteen. Two years. Nearly three. We met at the youth club and just seemed to get on with each other. So we started meeting up. It was so natural, so right. Of course things were difficult, right from the start. Not difficult for us. But difficult to admit.

Me and Steve, well, it's not the kind of thing people want to understand. Jokes are OK but the truth's a bit too real for comfort.

My mum really likes him. She's very keen for me to have friends. But she doesn't know how we feel about each other. It wouldn't occur to her. Sometimes I reckon I should tell her what's happening. I'd like her to know but it's hard to decide how she'd take it. She lives in a different world.

To be honest, I dunno what to do. Steve reckons I should move away to Manchester with him. It's a big city, I'd be able to get work of some kind. He's very insistent. I suppose he's right an' all. Once we're separated from each other things are bound to change. I don't wanna lose him.

But then there's my mum. She's waiting for another hip operation. Some days she can barely move at all. How can I leave her? Who else is gonna look after her?

There just don't seem to be any easy answers.

▽ Joan

(Paul's mother. She is sixty and has suffered from arthritis some time. Her husband died eight years ago and she lives in a small bungalow with her only son.)

What I say is, nothing's as bad as it could be. It's not the pain that annoys me so much as the frustration at not being able to do the things I'd always taken for granted. Even getting out of a chair is a major struggle. Doctor Morrison says that once I've had the operation I'll be leaping around again like a spring lamb. I'll settle for not having to walk with a frame. And it's hardly fair on Paul, having to fetch and carry all the time. He's a young man now. He should be able to have a life of his own.

Sometimes I find it hard to know what he wants. I told Hugh that we were a bit old to start a family. We married late, see, and by the time Paul came along I was already past forty. I'm not saying I regret having him, heaven forbid, but I wish I'd been younger and more able to understand him. We get on nicely enough but we never seem to talk. Not really talk. I don't know what he's thinking.

If only he'd get out more. He worries about me too much. I've got my frame and the bleeper in case of emergencies. I'm still fairly capable of looking after myself. Maybe after the operation I'll be able to convince him. Lord knows, hanging around here is no place for a young lad like him.

At least he's started to make friends. Steve's a nice young man. He comes round quite often. He's always bringing me chocolates and bowls of fruit. 'His older woman', he calls me. One day, he says, he's going to whisk me off to an island paradise and have his wicked way with me! He's so incorrigible! It's a pity he's going away in the autumn. Paul needs more friends like that, he needs to get out of himself. Have a few adventures.

Yes, maybe after the operation things will change.

▼ Stephanie

(Stephanie is fourteen. Her mother died when she was nine and since then she and her father have lived alone together.)

It's not right. That's all there is to it.

We've got along OK by ourselves. I do the cooking when I get home from school, Dad does the washing up. We've got our own system for cleaning the house – I'm in charge of the kitchen and bathroom and he does the lounge and hallways. In the evening we like to watch telly or play cards. We're happy enough. Why does he want it all to change?

I suppose it started a few months ago when Dad joined his club. I didn't know what it was really, but every Wednesday he'd go out after dinner while I stayed here on my own. I didn't mind. It was nice to have the place to myself for a while and I suppose it was also good that Dad got out and met new people.

Then one day last month over dinner he said we were having a visitor round. A friend of his, he said, who he'd met at the club. That was the night I realised something was going on, and that things were about to change.

'This is Moira', he said. I was a bit surprised – I'd expected someone older. She seemed nice enough though. She had good taste in clothes: a white shirt dress with a wide black belt and matching shoes. Very trendy. And she was very friendly to talk to. I decided I liked her. But later, I'd been upstairs playing records and when I came down there they were sitting together on the sofa, holding hands. And the way they behaved after that. I mean, she could've been my older sister and there she was hugging and kissing my dad. I didn't know what to say or do.

Moira came round quite a lot after that. A couple of days ago I got back from school and she was in the kitchen getting dinner ready. Dad'd given her the key, without even telling me. She said she was doing something special. Carbonara. Spaghetti with cheese and bits of bacon in it. I mean, me and Dad, we hate spaghetti.

Now Dad tells me she's going to be moving in, and they hope to get married once they've 'won her parents round'.

But I mean it's just not right. How can he marry her? She's only twenty-two. He should find someone his own age.

▼ Nicholas

(Stephanie's father. He is forty-one. His wife died five years ago.)

There was no warning. Brain haemorrhage. Cassie had always suffered with her migraines but we never imagined . . . The doctors said it was rare that it should have happened so suddenly. As if that was any consolation.

The first few months were almost unbearable. Life seemed so vast and empty. So cold. I didn't know if I wanted to go on. But I had to. Stephanie had to be looked after. So I did my work and looked after my daughter. I went through the motions.

Stephie coped well with her mum's death. We talked a lot. She wanted to be reassured that her mother had gone to a better place and was happy, that everything was all right really. As Stephie grew older, we worked out a rota for the house. She got involved with the shopping and cooking. That certainly helped. I'd always found preparing food difficult. It was something Cassie and I used to do together.

Time went by and I started to face facts. Cassie was gone. One day Stephie would also leave and make her own life. I began to feel trapped, sitting at home night after night playing cards and watching TV. And when Stephie was in bed, all alone with thoughts that didn't seem to lead anywhere.

So I started going to the club. 'Companions.' We met once a week in a room at the Carpenters Arms, and there were other outings to the cinema and theatre and social functions. It took me a long time to decide to join. When I first saw the ad in the paper I thought 'No way, not a singles club, I'm no misfit'. Bit I knew that companions were just what I needed at the time. What was there to lose?

The members were really nice people, if a bit timid perhaps. Quite often there'd be a group of us sat round a table at the Arms all waiting for a conversation to begin. Some were widowed like me, others divorced, some just unattached, lonely, new to town. A complete cross-section of people with one thing in common – the need for company and friendship.

I'd been going a few weeks when Moira joined. She was quite different from the others. Very lively, outgoing. I wouldn't say I fell for her immediately, mainly because I didn't feel capable of thinking in those terms. But we got on well. We seemed to spend most of our time at the club sitting together, chatting about this and that. Yes, she was a lot younger than me. But it didn't seem to matter. In fact, Moira thinks that's part of the attraction. 'Older men have more to say for themselves, more to reveal', she says.

We started meeting away from the club. She came round and met Stephie. They hit it off immediately. That was a great relief. I was afraid Stephie might feel threatened having another woman around, but if she does she certainly hasn't said so. Moira's parents are proving more of a problem. She's still living at home and as far as they're concerned she's still their little girl. The idea of going with a man old enough to be her father is practically unthinkable! It is making life a bit difficult but Moira swears they'll come round eventually. That's one of the things I admire about her – she's not prepared to let problems get the better of her.

She believes that if you keep going eventually you'll get there.

And she's right. We will get there. I'm very excited about her moving in with Stephie and me. I've lived inside myself for too long. At last life is beginning to seem valuable again.

▼ Moira

(Moira is twenty-two. She works in the advertising depart-ment of a local newspaper and lives at home with her parents.)

I'd been engaged to Jonathan for two years, and we'd been going out together ever since leaving school. Mum and Dad thought the world of him. 'A very personable young man', Mum called him. But they didn't know the other side. I suppose he was just a kid really. If he didn't get his own way he became intolerable. It wasn't until last summer, when we went on holiday together, that I finally realised what he could be like. Being alone together for two weeks, we seemed to spend most of the time squabbling. He wanted to hang round the hotel beach all day, I wanted to see a few of the sights. Majorca has some very attractive villages and countryside, if you've got the imagination to go and look. One day I decided to go off on my own. He couldn't take that. As far as he was concerned, if I didn't want to be with him I must've had another bloke hidden away somewhere. He threatened to hit me. I made the peace for the rest of the holiday, then once we got home I broke off the engagement. Mum and Dad tried to dissuade me, but I was determined not to go through with the marriage for the sake of other people. Life means more to me than that.

I met Nicholas on a whim I suppose. A friend of mine had told me about the singles club. I was unattached. It was a laugh really. I wanted to meet new people, have a good time, get Jonathan out of my system. You see, I still cared for him. Part of me still thought . . . but that was foolish. We weren't right for each other. End of story.

Nicholas was totally different. Very quiet, thoughtful. And he knew how to listen. I felt I could talk to him, whereas with Jonathan words were just things that filled in the pauses. He told me about his wife, and his daughter. He'd been through so much, suffered so much. In an odd way maybe that was the attraction. He knew about life, the bad as well as the good. I knew quite quickly that Nicholas was the kind of man I'd been waiting for. A person, not an ego.

Mum and Dad are horrified. They can't see beyond the age difference. I haven't told them I'm about to move in with Nicholas. They're going to find out soon enough. I'm not sure Stephie's too pleased about me either. When Nicholas is around she's all sweetness and light but when we're alone together, I don't know, there's a coldness, a resentment. It'd be silly to imagine things are going to be easy. But I know what I want, and that's what counts most.

▽ Kevin

(Kevin has recently left school. He works on a window-cleaning round and still lives at home. Here he talks about his relationship with Janine.)

I met her when I was cleaning windows. Love at first wipe, you could say. It was a posh house and all – big, with a large garden overlooking the park. Anyway, I was doing the windows and there she was, eating breakfast. Then she invites me in for coffee. We gets chatting. Her dad's a doctor and her mum 'lectures' as she calls it. Her older brother moved away last year so during her holidays she's got the whole place to herself. I mean, it's crazy really. All that space for one out-of-work student. Only she says she's not out of work. She's writing her book. Don't know what it's about. Strange that. From the moment I met her Janine's always had loads to say for herself but the book never gets talked about. A regular secret.

What attracted me first was her openness, I suppose. Plus her looks, of course. I don't think I've ever seen anyone so beautiful. Good job I didn't first see her when I was cleaning the upstairs windows – I'd've fallen off my ladder! And she makes life so interesting. I never bothered much at school. Waste of time my dad used to say. But with Janine, learning things is exciting. Different music. Art galleries. Films with subtitles. At first I thought it'd be dead boring, but she knows how to make it interesting. 'You see, Kev', she says, 'you're not as stupid as you like to think'. Works two ways of course. I'm teaching her to play snooker. And she likes getting out and meeting my mates. I was a bit worried about people meeting her at first. You know what they're like – anything different and they switch off. But most of the time it's OK.

My dad's the real problem. He can't stand Janine. 'Posh cow', he calls her. That's a laugh. It's got nothing to do with being a girl from The Parks. If she was white, he'd be falling over himself. Janine tells me not to get uptight about it. 'It's his problem, not ours', she says. But you can't help feeling ashamed. Janine's parents are so friendly, so understanding. If only Dad could be a bit more like that.

▽ Janine

(Janine is a student, studying English and politics. Her parents moved to Britain from the West Indies long before she was born.)

England is my home. It's the only country I've lived in, the only place I really know.

If I was white I wouldn't have to keep saying that. All the assumptions people make wouldn't apply if my parents were European. Everybody's different, but I sometimes think people can only cope by pretending we're all alike. Being black spoils the pretence. But I am different, they'd better get used to the fact. I don't want to be a cardboard cut-out. I want to be me.

It's not easy. My parents have very fixed ideas. Be a teacher, my dad says, it's a good profession. Doesn't he read the papers? My mum says she wants me to be happy but their idea of happiness is a nice house, and money, and all that goes with it. The good life. I'd love to go to Jamaica. I know so little about my background, the place my parents came from, the culture that I should still feel a part of. But my parents never go back. They're here, they've made it. How can they think like that?

They don't like Kevin at all. Of course, they're far too polite and civilised to admit it outright. Whenever he comes round they make him feel welcome. But I can tell. It's not his colour they object to. A nice white boy, what could be better? It would be a way of showing how British they'd become. But he's a window cleaner and he talks about football and wears old sweatshirts. Not 'one of us'. I've had a few rows with them about it. They're so stuck up, they don't know how to treat people for who they are. I love Kev. I love him because he's prepared to be himself. He's honest and open. And he's interested in discovering new things. That's what life's about, after all – being open about yourself and ready to accept new ideas. If only my parents could see that.

Barry

(Barry is a popular lad with both teachers and pupils and is in his fourth year at secondary school.)

If there's one thing I like about school it's the trips we have. Went to France when I was in the first year, right laugh that was. Then camping in Wales, rained every day. We've been cycling, sailing and a couple of days in London. I'll say one thing for the teachers at our school they do organise some good days out. Take last term. There was this trip for the first years to the zoo. Teacher comes along and says there was a few spare seats left on the coach and did we want to go. She says us being fourth years we could help sort 'em out at the zoo. 'Right on', I says to her, and me and me mate had the seats.

   When we got there we had to look after a couple of these first years. Place was real busy with school parties . . . some in proper school uniform . . . dead posh. These two sprogs (that's what we call first years at our school) wanted to see the chimps so off we went . . . one of 'em starts taking the micky out of the chimps. You know the sort of thing, walking round with his arms down by his sides, rolling from side to side and making chimp noises. One chimp looks dead miserable. The more this kid makes the chimp noises, the more miserable looks the chimp. The chimp then picks up a lump of muck . . . this kid copies him and his mate is laughing so much he is almost crying. Next moment . . . splat! The chimp throws the lump of muck and it hits this lad straight between the eyes, all over his face and clothes. He smells terrible and it is his turn to look miserable. The chimp mimes the lad and copies his actions. Who's got the last laugh now?

Never take the micky out of a chimp. He'll make a monkey out of you.

Lyn

(Lyn's dad plays cricket, a sport which Lyn finds very boring.)

I heard this voice come from the front room. 'Left foot forward . . . good balance . . . play down the line.' It sounded like my dad, but not being too sure I went to take a look. Through the open window I could see him, with his silly blue sun hat on, socks tucked into his trousers, waving a cricket bat about. He was so much into his own world that he didn't even notice I was there.

'Not too much bottom hand', he said in a kind of peculiar whisper. I could feel the giggles coming on. 'Dad what are you doing?' 'Nothing', he said hurriedly hiding the bat and pulling the socks out of his trousers.

'You were talking to yourself, I heard you . . . "play down the line . . . not too much bottom hand".' 'I was . . . reading.' 'Crap', I blurted out, realising too late what I'd said. 'Lyn . . . how many times have I told you about swearing . . .' But by now I knew I was on to something. 'You've bought a new cricket bat haven't you?' He stopped dead in his tracks. 'What?', he asked feebly. 'You heard.' 'How did you know?'

I didn't need to answer that one. He was in a tight corner and he knew I knew it. 'Wait till Mum finds out she'll go spare . . . and don't try and bribe me to keep quiet about it . . . no, I don't want extra pocket money this week.'

After all I have my principles.

His hand was in his pocket searching for loose change and brought out a silver coin. 'Not for fifty pence at least.' I couldn't hold back the giggles and ran off through the door and down the garden path.

Now you might think I'm being pretty mean to my dad, but you don't know him. Mum and I have got a kind of pact about his cricket. When I was a tiny baby I used to have to go to watch his silly matches. It was like that for years, and it was *Megaboring*! My mum used to do the cricket teas. Then one day, when they had all turned their noses up at her wholemeal flan, she decided enough was enough. 'Would all you men come and stand around for hours and make our teas if we had an all women's team?', she asked. 'I know you bloody well wouldn't. And that's why I've made my last cricket tea. If you want any teas, do them yourselves.'

It caused quite a stir in the cricket club you can be sure of that. But she was right, dead right and I admire her for doing it.

5
Viewpoints

Sally

(Sally is six years old.)

She's evil. I know. Dale Clark climbed over her wall once and he got a big cut right down his arm. She's got a knife, I bet. She cuts people up an' sees their blood.

An' she's got a beard. An' she wears old socks. An' boots. I bet she goes out at night an' kicks people. She shouted at Moira McAllister. She did. She said the eff word. I heard her.

My mum says she's a dirty old woman. She never washes. I bet she's never had a bath in a hundred million years. That's why nobody likes her. She's smelly an' ugly an' she makes up spells so terrible things happen. She's like a witch only she hasn't got a black cat. That's cos cats wouldn't go near her.

When you go past her house you can hear screaming. An' you have to run past the door quick or else you'll get a spell put on you an' all your teeth'll fall out.

One day she'll die an' we'll have a big party. an' then everything'll be all right.

▽ Jill

(Sally's mother.)

Quite frankly, I think it's time she moved out. For her own sake as much as anyone else's. It's absurd, one old woman living in a big old house like that. She's in no fit state to look after it. I mean, the curtains are brown with dirt, the garden's overgrown and the house itself can't have been painted this side of the war. Surely it's not good for her, locked away by herself. She doesn't have any relatives, you see. No one to look after her.

From what I've heard she used to be very well off. Her late husband was a government official of some sort. Some say he was a spy who fled the country just before his treachery was discovered. Anyway, she'd amassed quite a fortune, then went off to Monte Carlo or somewhere and frittered nearly all of it away on the gambling tables. At least, that's the story Mr Hubbard at the grocery told me and I suppose he should know – he delivers her groceries to the house each week.

Strangely enough, I've never actually met her myself. Sally's seen her a few times. She doesn't look after her appearance from what I hear. The children all think she's some sort of witch. You have to laugh! They've got such wild and vivid imaginations. Lord knows where they get their ideas from.

The best thing the old lady could do is sell up and find herself a nice little rest home. Give the house to someone with the money and energy to look after it. As Mrs Brown pointed out at the last Residents Council meeting, the place really does stick out like a sore thumb. Yes, it would benefit everyone if she'd only see reason. Trouble is, old people are so stuck in their ways, aren't they?

▽ Emily

(Emily is eighty-four. She lives alone in the big house she first moved into when she was married, fifty-seven years ago. She has been widowed for nearly twenty years and her two sons both live abroad.)

Oh dear. They're still out there. I wish they'd go away. I must post this letter. How can I leave the house if there are people around?

One can't trust a soul these days. Not even small children, I've seen them, creeping into my garden. If I tell them to go away they just laugh and shout names. Don't they realise how frightening it all is? Why do they haunt me so? What have I ever done to them?

If only Gerald would answer my letters. I keep writing asking him what I should do but he hasn't replied since Christmas. And that was just a few words on a card. I know he's very busy over there in America but I would so like to hear from him. Or from Norman. Still, I know what Norman thinks. He wants me to sell the house and go out and live near them. But that's not for me. I went over to see him a few years ago. Far too hot and noisy for my liking. And really, a son of mine running a gambling casino! It's not something one wants to be reminded of.

No. This is our home. This is where I belong. But if only it wasn't so frightful. If only I could get out once in a while without fear of getting attacked. Dear me, I wish I knew what I could do about it.

▼ Val

(Val has known Shirley and Terry for many years.)

Shirley and I went to school together and we've been friends ever since. I was godmother at Terry's christening and cried at the funeral when the two were left without father and husband. I'd have expected the two of them to grow even closer after that tragedy but somehow it hasn't happened.

Shirley was the devoted wife and mother. Frank's tea was put on the table at half past five every evening, the house was immaculate and she spent all her time with her growing son. Then her husband dies. Her life will be finished I thought and I spent the next few months making cups of tea and playing the social visitor.

But that part didn't last long and the next thing she's off to college to make a new life for herself. I don't blame her for that, she was always very clever at school and there was some special recruiting scheme round here to cope with a desperate shortage of Maths and Science teachers. Frank had an excellent life insurance so there are no money problems.

And yet . . . it's as if I've never really known Shirley. All those years . . . she's somehow a very different person now. It's Terry I feel sorry for. Last week I popped in to see Shirley; she was out of course but Terry was there by himself. I cooked his dinner for him and he asked me to eat with him. Poor lad, I could tell something was wrong. He wouldn't say too much to start with. I said to myself 'Val, if the lad doesn't want to tell you, well that's up to him'. But tell me he did. He had been trying to find a few papers of his own and had found some college form to show that his mother was going away in a few weeks time for a full week away. Some kind of field trip apparently. 'Well that will be nice for her', I said. 'But she hasn't told me, not a word', said Terry and I could see he was close to tears. He may be seventeen and a big lad but that boy was very upset.

He pleaded with me not to say anything to Shirley and of course I haven't. But . . . what has happened to her? How can she treat her own son like that, at a time when he needs her so much? That's not like Shirley. Not the Shirley I know.

▼ Shirley

(Shirley is Terry's mother and has just started her first year of a polytechnic teaching course.)

If somebody had said to me a while ago, 'Shirley you'll be a college student', I'd have laughed at them. And now as I sit in this library surrounded by all these books I still don't quite believe it sometimes. The fact is I feel alive, like breathing in the air for the first time, and at my age, well that's not bad.

I've just had a tutorial and George – that's the name of the tutor – is really great. We sat out on the garden seat in the courtyard in the old part of the building with a coffee and chatted about my last assignment. Not that George seemed very worried about it. He said I showed 'considerable potential as a mature student . . . with a logical and perceptive view'. Then he asked me about myself and how I was finding the course. All the tutors here are so helpful and friendly.

We've got five mature students in our group, then twelve people who have come straight from school and two more in their mid-twenties. We get on so well. Everybody was apprehensive at first, but nobody seems brilliant and we all support each other. Next month there is a full week away on a field trip in Wales: 'Environmental Issues' that's called. Should be good.

Then of course there's the teaching part. We've started to go into schools in groups, to observe and then work with three or four children. Next term it's the actual teaching practice itself. That I'm dreading; can already feel a lump in my throat. Only at times like that do I really wonder if I've made the right decision.

▼ Terry

(Terry is seventeen and has just come home to an empty house.)

Not again! She's always out. It's great talking to a chair. I'll bet it's cornish pasties again. I wouldn't mind, but if it's one thing I hate it's cornish pasties. I need a decent meal when I get in, not having to scramble about in the freezer and cook my own.

Do you know where she is? Have a guess? Down that bloody college, that's where. Said she'd be early tonight, no lectures on this afternoon, that's what she said. And what do I find when I get in? An empty, dirty, cold house waiting for me.

She's a student, my forty year old mother is a student. I think she's cracking up. A couple of years ago it was folding bits of paper to look like birds, the year before that pottery. This year teaching, training to be a science teacher, my mother – what a laugh. I wouldn't mind but she's wasting her time, she won't last the course. First bit of real teaching, by herself in front of a class of kids and that will be that. I know her after all these years. Tears, histrionics, more panic and she'll be packing in that course.

I suppose I should be pleased with the prospect. At least there'll be some decent food on the table. Only I'm not. I'm dreading it. I shall have to stay calm, put my arm round her wipe away her tears and lie like hell. Why can't she be just like a normal mother? It's not much to ask, is it?

6
Problems

▽ Roger

(Roger is a temporary supply teacher working in a very large secondary school.)

Angela look at me when I'm talking to you. All the rest of the class have managed to write something and you haven't. Why? Why Angela? Just look at this book . . . your book . . . go on look at it. Open the book Angela . . . come on . . . very well I'll open it for you. Well, what do you see? I'll tell you what I see. But I'd like to hear from you . . . well? There is not one piece of work since I've been taking you . . . not one word of writing . . . just blank pages. I just don't understand you Angela . . . you've always got something interesting to say in class when I ask you. But now you are choosing to say nothing, not one word. I've had enough of this Angela I can see I'm wasting my time trying to reason with you. There are twenty-nine other people in this class, they need attention as well. Don't you ever think about them? Obviously not. I'm already late for my next lesson which is over in upper school. I'm going to pass this on to your head of house. Perhaps you will be able to explain to her what's going on. You'll probably be seeing her tomorrow. You can go now, go to your next lesson.

▽ John

(John Parrish is Angela's father.)

Yes Barbara . . . I know she can't read . . . I do know she's twelve years old and you expect a daughter of yours to know the basics . . . and you feel ashamed that she can't . . . you've told me often enough . . . but don't you see it's so difficult. She's been in and out of that hospital ever since she was tiny . . . or haven't you even noticed that fact? You've buried yourself in your work . . . you wouldn't know what had happened to her. Perhaps you tried to pretend she wasn't your daughter. Like an ostrich with its head in the sand. We can't put any more pressure on her now. What does it matter if she can't read . . . so long as she's alright. Just give her time . . . that's all she needs right now . . . our trust and love and time.

▽ Barbara

(Barbara is Angela's mother and is telephoning Angela's school.)

Hello . . . is that Greenway Comprehensive School? . . . this is Mrs Parrish . . . the mother of Angela Parrish . . .

she was due to start at your school last week . . . on the
first day of term . . . sorry . . . its Parrish . . . P – A . . .
oh I see, well could I speak to the lower school office?
. . . no I'm sorry I can't phone back later . . . could
you make sure they receive the message then please . . .
Parrish . . . P–A–R–R–I–S–H . . . Angela Parrish . . . .
yes that's right . . . yes in the first year . . . no we didn't
receive the details from her junior school . . . yes . . . I
don't know how long it will be, I'm afraid she's still in
hospital. She missed quite a lot of her junior and infant
school time. We were hoping she might have been able
to start on the first day of term but I'm afraid this is not
now possible. No I'm afraid I don't know quite how long
it will be . . . Yes I certainly will . . . thank you.

▽ Elizabeth

*(Elizabeth and Angela were at the same school together.
Although they did know each other very well they have met
up again after leaving school and Elizabeth has offered to
help Angela make a belated start to learn to read and write.
Angela is now aged seventeen.)*

I've had this brilliant idea. I've been down the library.
You should have seen me . . . sitting on this tiny chair in
the kids quiet corner . . . knees up to me chin, fighting
with the four year olds for the best books. Talk about
grievous bodily harm. Why do they all want the books
with Thomas the Tank engine? I ask you Thomas the
bloody tank engine. I go in . . . creep past the librarian
. . . pick up a kid's alphabet book and I think . . . this is

where we'll start . . . Angela and me and the reading . . . next moment I've got some snotty-nosed kid running her fingers through me hair . . . then they all want a go . . . fight breaks out and I'm in the middle of it. I tell you what if they're short of contenders for the boxing championship of the world they just need to go down to that library – little sods. Then I hear 'Silence . . . silence . . . can we have silence!' It's the voice . . . the librarian voice. Kids ignore it and carry on doing Dracula impressions. The voice walks over and screams 'SILENCE'. I manage to breathe again; as she walks away one of the kids blows this massive raspberry. Result? Victory to the boxing contenders, I'm chucked out of the library . . . called a weirdo . . . kids follow me down the street like the pied piper of bloody Hamlin . . . but I managed to get *My First Book of the Alphabet*. Shall we start to read it now?

Tanya

(Tanya is fourteen. She has a history of stealing from friends and family. She has recently been put into care, rejected by her parents.)

I wasn't supposed to stay here. That's what I was told. Three weeks I've been here now. It's up to me what happens, they say. It's what I do that makes the difference. But it isn't. Rita's the one who makes things happen.

At first I got on really well with Rita. She's a bit older than me and she'd been told to look after me, show me round. I thought I could trust her. We're both in the same situation, why shouldn't I trust her? Rita said she'd look after some things for me – my walkman, magazines, my steel comb. She said we weren't allowed things like that and she'd keep them safe. Rita really helped me the first few days – told me how to behave with different people, what best to say. We'll be out of here in no time, she said.

Then one day she changed. Moody. I didn't know what was wrong. Then at dinner she started screaming at me. Right in front of everyone. I was a 'thieving bitch', she said, I was sly and evil. I didn't know what she meant. Mrs Freeman took her away and then a few minutes later I was called for.

In the bedroom, Mrs Freeman and Rita were waiting for me. Rita wasn't shouting now; she sat on the bed crying. The pillow had been pulled back from the bed. Underneath was my walkman, smashed and crumpled. Mrs Freeman wanted to know what I had to say for myself. Wasn't I ashamed to mistreat a friend's property like this? But it was my walkman. I was the one who'd been abused. I tried to explain but Mrs Freeman just stood looking at me, cold, unbelieving. 'You've done things like this before, haven't you Tanya?' she said. Behind Mrs Freeman I could see Rita's face. The tears had gone, she was grinning broadly.

Bob

(Bob is visiting his daughter in hospital.)

They don't tell you much in here. I've just been to see Vicky, she seems to be much better, but I wonder. A nine year old doesn't cough up blood without something's wrong. There are five more like Vicky in there and nobody is saying anything.

Last week Vicky and a few of her friends went to play on this bit of waste ground where we live. It was Saturday afternoon. Next thing I knew the police were round and Vicky was in hospital. Seems there's some kind of dump up there and drums of chemicals just lying around. It used to be old allotments up there, I didn't know nothing about no chemicals.

It seems these chemicals is highly dangerous giving off fumes and the kids played near 'em. They said they was roped off and some kind of notice put up, but kids that age take no notice of things like that. Besides there's nowhere else much to play on, not for kids round here.

They've put it all in the papers and we've had reporters round asking all kind of questions. They reckon there's been some kind of fiddle down the council and they've arrested some bloke. It says he knew really these chemicals were deadly but took a back hander to keep quiet about it. The stuff they dumped came from France. One of the newspaper fellows said it's happening all over the world, even worse in Africa. Kids will die by the thousands because a world doesn't know what to do with its tons and tons of toxic waste, he said. Reckoned I could sue the council for thousands.

That's as maybe. All I want is for Vicky to come home and the doctors to tell me there's not lasting harm on her health. And she'll not play no more near that tip. I'll make sure of that.

Samita

(Samita is in her third year at a comprehensive school.)

They called her 'Fatty'. It seemed a bit of a joke to start with. We were in the first year together, not the same class, but friends. She didn't mind too much then, but since the third year it's got so much worse. If we went down town I felt so bad. The clothes shops were terrible. She used to tell me that she had a thirty-four inch waist and said that the people in the shops were laughing at her. She could never find anything to fit her and for the last year or so she wouldn't go shopping with me.

We used to be in the same group for games and she dreaded swimming. She'd stand there with her arms crossed trying to cover up her figure. Her shorts were huge and as for PE knickers, well she refused to do the lessons if she had to wear them.

As for boys, well I suppose that was the start of it all. She really liked this lad in the second year and some of her form got to know. They gave her and the lad hell. 'If you want a real girl, Fatty's waiting', they say to him. 'She wants to sit on your knee.'

It was not that she seemed to eat much, not at school anyway, but by the beginning of the third year she was very fat. Then she stopped eating. She never told anybody much about it. Her Mum didn't even know. I don't know how she managed it, but she did. She began to lose weight, you could see it. Her clothes hung on her. But still the kids at school wouldn't let it drop. 'Look at Fatty . . . on a diet are we . . . all because of love . . . you'll have to lose a lot more yet before you can sit on his knee Fatty, you'll still crush him to death.'

She began to miss days at school, she fainted in assembly and I really began to worry about her. Still she lost weight. I went round to her house to see her and her

Mum said she'd got an████xia, and that she was too tired for me to see her.

Last night they took her to hospital and she's now in a coma. Her life is in the balance, they told us at school. The teacher also explained about anorexia and how many people of Jane's age it affects each year. Even those morons in her class looked sorry. But it's too late now. Why couldn't she just be Jane, herself in her own right instead of 'Fatty', always 'Fatty'.

Digga

(Digga is in his last year of school, and leader of the Protection Society.)

Well, it's a service that's what it is. You need some homework done, I arrange it. Want a sick note? I'm the bloke to see. Lost your PE kit? Need to borrow 50p for dinner? You got a problem, you come to me. That's what the Protection Society is all about.

Only you see, we can't do it for nothing. These things take money. I mean, 10p a day. Not gonna hurt you is it? It's like insurance really. You give me 10p, I see you're protected. Then when you've got a problem, you come to me and for a small fee I fix it for you. You can hire a pair of swimming trunks for as little as 25p per day. I mean, can't be bad, eh? Why risk bringing your own trunks to school? Everything gets nicked round here.

Even if you don't want to make use of our services, you still have the peace of mind that protection brings. Let's be honest, kids can get hurt in a place like this. They can get pushed down staircases, attacked in the corridor, hacked down on the football field. Why take the risk? Only 10p a day and you'll be safe from all that. Do yourself a favour, eh?

Nigel

(Nigel is thirty years old and lives alone in his small flat.)

The mouse is back.

I heard it last night as I lay in bed. I heard it scuttling away behind the skirting board. This morning I found that the rubbish bag in the kitchen had been eaten into. Just a small hole, but a hole nevertheless. Why does it always pick on me?

Of course, I'm assuming it's the same mouse. I'm assuming there's still only the one. For all I know it might have brought its chums along. There might well be a whole nest of them hidden under the floorboards.

This time, something drastic must be done.

Don't get me wrong, I have nothing against mice. I mean them no harm. But there's something about them – their manner, the way they scurry about, their beady little eyes. It's nonsense I know. They're not dangerous, I know that. But all the same, I can't help it. I can't bear the sight or sound of them.

I've tried peaceful persuasion. I've cleared all the empty cans and rubbish bags from under the sink. I've thrown out my collection of old newspapers. I've started to keep the flat spotless. And what good has it done? The mouse is back.

The man in the shop was very helpful. He showed me how the spring mechanism worked and with the tip of his pencil demonstrated its efficiency. 'Instantaneous, of course', he told me, 'breaks the backbone on impact. They don't feel a thing. Very humane'. I didn't take much convincing.

I mean, I'm not the first person to lay a trap. People do it all the time, don't they? People lay traps. They put down poison. Some lie in wait with airguns and old boots. I'm not doing anything that hasn't been done a million times before.

I'm doing it because I have to. I'm doing it because there is no choice. I can't function properly under these conditions. It's my flat, isn't it? I have every right to protect myself.

You can understand that, can't you?

7
Gina

▽ Patricia

(Patricia is fifteen years old, a classmate of Gina's.)

She was odd. You know, quiet. You couldn't really talk
to her. We sat together sometimes. But she never had
two words to say for herself. I mean, it's not as if she
was a swot or anything like that. Most of the time she just
scribbled drawings in her books. Well, I say drawings but
they were mostly just squiggles and lines.

   We used to call her 'Deadhead'. It was just for a laugh.
I don't think it bothered her. I don't think anything bothered her, know what I mean? She was never really there,
you see. Never a part of anything. Maybe 'Deadhead' was
the wrong nickname. I reckon that was the only place she
really existed – in her head.

   Yeh, she was weird all right.

▽ Margaret

(Gina's mother.)

I don't know why she did it. If I could even begin to understand . . . But I can't. There's no reason. No logic.

She used to get such strange ideas into her head. When she was nine she became obsessed with the idea that she was adopted. We tried to reassure her. I gave her a copy of her birth certificate. But she was convinced we weren't her parents. Why was she like that? We gave her as much as we could. We brought her up properly didn't we? Frank worshipped her. He did. She meant the world to him. I mean, I can't believe . . . I don't know why she says half the things she says. There's something cold inside her. An emptiness or a pain or something. I wish there was something I could do.

She was a lovely child. When she was younger she was so lively and loving. We had such wonderful times together, the three of us. I suppose being an only child she was rather spoilt. Sundays at the seaside. Ice creams and sandcastles. Rides on the dodgems. If only she could have stayed like that. Stayed as eight years old. But as she got older it all changed. She'd lock herself away in her room. Frank'd go up and try and talk to her. But it didn't help. She just retreated more and more into herself. We were helpless to know what to do.

And then, well, what can I say? Whatever else, she was never a violent girl. How could she do that? Why?

▽ Gina

(Gina is fifteen. She is very withdrawn, keeps herself to herself.)

He's not my real father. My mother says he is, but I know differently. I've always known. I think he was probably a lodger or something like that, and then when my real dad was out of the way he just took over. It happened when I was very young, of course. I don't remember exactly what took place. But I know that's what happened.

I liked him to begin with because he was funny. At night, he tucked me in and told me stories. He told jokes all the time. And he used to cuddle me really tight. I didn't mind that. The cuddling was all right. But you see he wasn't my real father and cuddling was never enough. Cuddling was just the start.

It wasn't nice what happend. I don't talk about it. It's my business. I mean, it's not the kind of thing I want to remember. Best forgotten. It's finished now.

I suppose my mum must've known what was going on. I suppose she just didn't care. Doesn't matter. I can look after myself.

I was getting breakfast. Cutting the bread. And he was reading the paper. 'Look at her', he said, showing me the girl in the paper. 'Only sixteen', he said, 'just like you.' And he laughed. And I told him not to say things like that to me, but he just laughed. And then he got up and started squeezing me. I said he'd better not do that or something'd happen. 'Must be my lucky day then', he said and kept squeezing and touching.

I'd always known that once I got the chance I'd make him stop. And I did. I turned round and . . . made him stop.

The look on his face. The shock in his eyes. 'That's the last time you touch me', I said. And it was. He doesn't touch me anymore. I'm OK now. Should've done it years ago.

▽ Dr Ryder

(A psychoanalyst.)

The evidence points to a sustained period of abuse and mistreatment. Gina has been subjected to acts of humiliation for a number of years. What is particularly striking is the manner in which she has coped with this. Her delusions of being adopted seem to be the start of other imaginings. Over the years she has created a whole fantasy world designed to block out the reality around her. This world has proved very hard to penetrate. She consistently refuses to reveal her thoughts. However, reading between the lines it seems that she believes herself to be a captive held by her father against her will, and that one day her 'true' father will return to look after her.

As to the event in question, it could be seen as an emotional flashpoint in an otherwise placid personality. However, there must remain the possibility that she deliberately planned the attack as a means of revenging herself and perhaps facilitating the return of her 'real' father.

Whether it was an act of provocation, or a planned action, the fact remains that Gina is at present in a state of psychological distress. She is certainly not capable of leading a normal, stable life and must be protected from herself.

▽ Rebecca

(Rebecca is twenty-three, and in her first year of English teaching.)

I should have done something. I mean, if I'd thought for a minute . . .

It began one morning after an English class I was taking. We'd been looking at a story of a young boy whose adopted parents die in a car crash and he runs away to find his real mum and dad. During the discussion I explained to the class that I'd been adopted. I like to feel I can confide in my pupils, show that I have experiences that relate to their work or even their own difficulties. Anyway, Gina stayed behind after the lesson and said she wanted to talk. I felt quite honoured. Gina Bryant was renowned in the staffroom as a girl who never said or did anything. Other members of staff had tried to communicate with her but all they got was a wall of silent indifference. And it was the same for me until that morning.

She told me that she was also adopted, but that her parents refused to admit it. I asked her why she thought this. She said she could only tell me if I promised not to repeat what she was about to say. Then she leaned over and whispered very quietly, as if we were co-conspirators or something. She explained about her father. About how he used to come to her room late at night. How he'd, well, forced himself on her. I couldn't believe what I was hearing. Such a horrific story but told so calmly. I know I shouldn't have kept the promise. But she seemed so in control, so matter of act. How could I betray her trust?

I did try to persuade her to tell someone in authority what was happening. But she got angry. 'It's my business.' She said that several times. She said she'd only told me because she thought I'd be interested. As far as she was concerned, this was just an extension of what had been discussed in class.

After that we used to talk quite often. She never said a word in class but afterwards she'd often stay for a chat. Her father was never mentioned again. She just seemed lonely, in need of someone who was prepared to listen. Someone who she felt she could trust.

Now, I feel so terrible. I could have done something. I could have helped. Maybe that's what she wanted, deep down. She wanted me to tell someone all about it. Looking back it seems so obvious. How could I make such a mistake?

8
Follow-up Work

Lisa

1 *Pair work*
  Choose the roles of Lisa's friends. Create a conversation between them: discussing Lisa's appearance.
    As a contrast to this, then take the roles of either:-
  – her parents, or
  – her school teachers,
  and create a second conversation.
    How do these conversations vary in their attitude towards the punk image?
2 *For discussion*
  Does our appearance tell us anything about our inner character? If you could meet Lisa when she is five years older how do you think she might look?

Charlotte

1 Make a chart of the food you have eaten in the last week.
  How much of the food was:
  – fresh vegetables?
  – meat?
  – microwaved from frozen?
  Share your own likes and dislikes of food as a whole class.
2 *Pair work*
  Consider the pressures upon a person when they decide to become a vegetarian. Create your own improvised scenes showing this pressure and how the person copes.

Here are a few suggestions you might try:
– Mum or Dad having to cook special meals just for you;
– a scene in a restaurant which doesn't offer a veg option;
– losing friends because of your eating choices.

3   *Group work*
To extend this work create a family meal time in which one member of the family is a vegetarian. You will need to use groups of three or four for this scene.

4   As a conclusion, consider what the pair work and group work has added to your understanding of what it is like to be a vegetarian.

Kieron   *Page 4*

1   *Try this game*
With the whole class sitting round in a circle, and with eyes closed, pass round several unidentified objects. After each one has been passed, write down what you think the object was. How many did you guess correctly?

   Consider what the game has taught you about the man Kieron described in his monologue.

2   With one volunteer taking either the role of Kieron or the man he describes, try a 'hot-seating activity' to establish the background details of the partially sighted man.

   To extend this further you may need to call upon several other roles to give you further details. These might include – members of the man's family, those working in support agencies relating to partially sighted people, and medical staff.

3   Using a few simple desks or chairs set up a house or room where the man lives. You can then create your own scenes set in the area you have created.

Kim   *Page 5*

1   *Group activity*
Explore your school and the nearby areas for provision for people confined to a wheelchair. Are there ramps for easy access? Are there places it is impossible for them to enter?

   What other provisions need to be made for the disabled in your school or community?

2   *Pair work*
Using Kim's monologue as a base, devise your own scenes to explore her story.

You might wish to consider the following areas:
- the relationship between her parents;
- the attitude of her teachers and schoolfriends; and
- Samina's situation.

3 Using the devised scenes together, can you add a simple story or narrative to build a drama documentary about Kim? Your narrative might need to move backwards and forwards in time in order to give an interesting story.

Katie

1 Using a series of still images create moments in the career of the group Katie has been following.
What do these still images tell you about their lifestyle?
Give the group an original name.
2 *Pair Work*
Taking the role of one of the group and a TV interviewer set up a scene in a television studio.
3 *For discussion*
Katie tells us she has now to change her image. What advice could you give her regarding this?
   After you have considered this, let someone take the role of Katie and respond to your advice.
4 *A final thought*
What caused the group to split up?

Credita

1 *Activity*
This monologue takes place in the year 2100. Try creating your own idea of what life will be like in the century after next. This can be organised as a group project, with people responsible for different aspects of life – e.g. education, work, home life, social life, government, etc. The aim is to create a world which you see as the logical progression of our own world. What aspects of this world do you think are most likely to have a strong influence on future life? It might be useful to begin by discussing within the group the overriding creed or philosophy that the future world will have (this could be just a phrase as it is in the monologue).
   Once you have created a clear picture of the world, think

about what the people living in that world might be like. This could involve writing your own monologues, or acting out scenes using the ideas you come up with in the project.

Afterwards, consider whether the future world you have created is one you would wish to live in. Does it represent your hopes or your fears for the future?

2 Consider Credita's monologue. What would you have done in her situation? What reason does the City have for making charity a crime?

3 The philosophy of Credita's world is 'Look After Yourself'. Discuss what you think are the slogans and philosophy of the world we live in.

Emma   *Page 9*

1 *For discussion*
   Do you think Emma's parents made a wise decision in allowing her to have the party? Emma uses the words 'You know, trust and all that'. What do you think she means?

2 *A whole class activity*
   Emma mentions the possibility of another 'little get together' next month. Imagine this to have taken place and that the 'unsavoury' gatecrashers vandalise the scene. Using the room you are in and with some care and thought set up the furniture to represent what the scene might look like. Do this as yourselves and not as the vandals. Once this has been done, stand to the sides of the room and discuss what you see.

   Imagine the vandals have left. Enter the scene as Emma's friends and decide what has to be done, through the action of the drama.

3 *Parental response*
   With two volunteers taking the roles of Emma's parents continue to run your scene. What is their response? Do they find out about the vandalism? Will they ever allow Emma to have another party?

4 *A few final thoughts*
   Why has this second party turned out so differently from the first? How might the problems have been avoided? Allow the two volunteers who have taken the roles of Emma's parents to have a few final thoughts concerning what has happened.

Beryl   *Page 10*

1 Consider some of the following facts about women and work during the Second World War:

* Between 1939 and 1943 the number of women in trade unions doubled.
* At the start of the war 17,000 women volunteered for the Land Army but only 5000 were taken on by farmers. By 1943 the situation had changed and there weren't enough recruits to go round.
* By 1944, women's average weekly earnings had increased by 60–90%.
* Creches and nurseries were set up for the children of working women.

What do these facts tell us about women's role in society during the war? After 1945, most jobs were given back to the men who returned from fighting. What difficulties do you think women would have faced after being used to earning their own living?

2 Make a list of what you think are the five most likely jobs for men to do, and the five most likely for women. What different skills or qualities do the jobs require? Are any of the jobs exclusive to one particular sex? If so, why?

3 Imagine that Beryl is a young woman nowadays, replying to a job ad for a farm labourer. What will the farmer's attitude be when she goes to see him? Act out a scene showing what she needs to do to get the job.

Dan	*Page 12*
Phyllis	*Page 13*

1 *In role*
Imagine the local newspaper is to publish a feature on Phyllis's appearance at the final of the pool competition. Taking either the roles of photographers, reporters, contestants or local inhabitants set up a series of interviews to find the background to the story.

If you are working for the newspaper, decide what the headline for the feature will be.

2 *For discussion*
How would you describe Dan's attitude to the pool competition?

Why do you think he contacted the local paper?

How long do you think he might have been landlord of 'The Plough'?

3 *Commentary*
In order to give you a clearer picture of the pool competition create your own commentary on either Phyllis's first match or final's night. These can be taped or videoed.

4 *Still pictures*
   Using a series of 'still pictures', create moments in Phyllis's life at various times before the pool competition. You could even go back as far as her childhood.

Rico
Page 15

1 *Game*
   Create a no man's land in the middle of the room. In the centre are two blindfolded guards. The rest of the group are refugees trying to cross the no man's land in ones and twos. If the guards hear someone crossing they call out 'Halt' and point to where they think the noise came from. Refugees who are captured in this way must sit down where they are until the end of the game. When the game is completed, count up the number of refugees who reached the other side. Was it difficult to get across?
2 As an extension of the game, role play a situation where the refugees who got across arrive in a foreign town. What problems might they face in terms of language difference, passport requirements, acceptance, etc? What action will the townspeople take when faced with a sudden influx of outsiders?
3 Read through the monologue and consider some of the following points:
   a) What do you feel is the tone and attitude of Rico as he tells his story?
   b) He says his sister is 'older and has a different life'. How do you think she survives in the city and why have they not stuck together?
   c) Do you believe Rico's father will come back and collect him? What kind of a life do you think the father has found in America?
4 In small groups, act out one of the following scenes:
   a) Rico and his friends return to their factory roof one night to find the factory owner waiting for them. He wants them to leave his property. Can they persuade him otherwise?
   b) Rico meets his sister one day by chance. How do they react to each other?
5 Consider what might happen to an abandoned child in this country. Why are the consequences so different for Rico?

Michael
Page 16

1 Imagine that this dispatch is for television. As a group devise and

act out a mime show which might accompany the first paragraph of the monologue. Try acting this out with the lines spoken aloud, or on tape. Consider the effect created. How did it make you feel? What ways forward for these people can you see?

2 Read through the monologue and consider the attitude of the reporter. What do you make of his 'nightmare'? Do you agree or disagree with his conclusions about the situation?

3 In small groups, adopt roles as members of an editorial team on a newspaper. This report has just been received. Yours is a popular paper, and has been heavily involved in various aid projects to help victims of famine and war. Decide as a group whether or not you intend to print the report as it stands. What effect do you think it will have on readers?

4 Write your own report reflecting your own opinions of third-world famine and showing what you think is the best way to deal with the problem.

Grant   *Page 17*

Tom   *Page 18*

Simeon   *Page 20*

1 *An action plan*
Working in small groups, read Grant's monologue carefully. Devise your own scene based upon Grant's description, trying to keep as close to his account as possible. Having done this, consider the incident. Is Grant telling the exact truth? If you were to show the incident from the viewpoint of Simeon how might your version be different?

Where do your sympathies lie as you watch your scene?

2 Ask two role players to take the roles of Tom and Simeon to try to show you what might have happened on one of Tom's visits. If this is difficult for the role players, you can stop the scene and suggest to them how they might act or what they might say. Perhaps you could try several visits to suggest the passing of time when Simeon is in prison.

What do these role plays add to your understanding of the situation?

Where does your sympathy lie now?

3 *A court room drama*
Imagine Simeon's case comes to court. This might be at the time of his arrest or after he has been in prison for some time. With a few simple changes to your room, set up the court and begin to

build the court case. You will need to hear evidence from several people. Your verdict can be taken by a jury or as a whole class vote.

4 *A final thought*
As a result of your courtcase decide what the future of Simeon is to be.

Cathy	*Page 22*
Rosemary	*Page 24*
Mike	*Page 24*

1 *A letter*
Imagine that Donna writes a letter to Cathy. It has no address written on it and is just pushed through her letter box.

Write your own version of the letter. Think about the details you would want to include and perhaps even the style of writing.

How will your letter end?

Share your letter with a friend. Talk about the mood Donna was in when she wrote the letter.

2 *Role play*
Using the letter as a prop, ask a volunteer to represent Donna.

As a whole class create a still picture at the moment Donna is writing the letter. Where is she? What is she thinking at this time? Can the person taking her role depict the thoughts that are going through her mind in a few words?

3 *Group work*
In small groups, act out a scene concerning the future in Donna's story *or* as a whole class take the roles of Donna's class. Run your scene beginning with Donna's re-entry into the classroom. What will happen? You may only want the scene to run for a very short time. Before you begin, check that the person taking the role of Donna is happy with the idea of this scene.

Tim	*Page 25*

1 *For discussion*
Why does Tim say 'Let me get it absolutely right . . . word perfect'?

Did he actually steal the wallet?

If you believe he didn't, why is he admitting to a theft he did not commit?

2 *Pair work*
  Act out your own version of the scene between Tim and his Head
  of Year. Will his story 'convince anybody'? What does your scene
  add to your understanding of the situation?
3 As an extension of this *either* devise a second scene when the
  Head of House is discussing the interview with fellow teachers *or*
  write a report of your interview with Tim as if you were the Head
  of House.
4 *A final thought*
  Is Tim the kind of person you would trust?

Lucy
Page 26

1 Working in small groups, consider the three questions Lucy asks
  at the beginning of the monologue. To develop this further open
  the discussion up to the whole class. Try to include details of any
  available evidence to support your own point of view, including
  personal experience or anecdote.
    Take a vote as a whole class upon the possibility of ghosts
  existing.
2 Conduct your own inquiry into Lucy's ghostly experience. You
  may perhaps need to call for evidence from the following:
  – Lucy,
  – various members of Lucy's family,
  – previous owners or occupants of the house,
  – experts in supernatural phenomena.
3 As a result of your inquiry, certain decisions, advice or actions
  may need to be taken. Put these into a drama form.
4 *A question*
  Is it possible the 'ghostly' happenings are some form of hoax or
  trick?
5 *Pair work*
  Create your own sound effects for ghostly noises. Tape them and
  play them back to the rest of the class. As you listen to them as a
  whole class, what kind of ghosts do the sounds suggest to you?

Kerrie
Page 28

1 Kerrie has never told her close friends or family about this
  incident. Why does it still seem so terrible to her? Are there any

secrets that you have never told anyone? Try and list reasons why people have and keep secrets.

2 *Pair work*
Act out the scene in the shop, showing what you think would have happened if Kerrie had owned up about the winegums.

3 It is sometimes said that people nowadays are expert liars; no one tells the truth unless they have to. As a group, discuss whether or not you agree with this. Is there a difference between truth and honesty?

4 Develop a piece of drama entitled 'I Never Done It!'. What images does this phrase conjure up?

Hannah   *Page 29*

1 *Pair work*
Try this improvisation in pairs. A is sitting on a park bench. B, a stranger, enters and starts a conversation with A. Before the scene begins B decides whether s/he is a lonely person who wants friendship or is a dangerous attacker. B's objective is to persuade A to trust him/her enough to be invited home for tea. A's objective is to work out whether B can be trusted. The scene ends when B is invited back, or when A walks away from the situation.

   Afterwards, tell each other what your thoughts and intentions were. Did B's behaviour give any clues to his/her objective?

2 In the monologue Hannah gets rid of the attacker. She is alone in her house. Why do you think he did not attack her? Make a list of what you think are the best ways to prevent an attack like this happening.

3 Consider the role of the attacker. Try and build up a picture of what you think he is like. Why does he attack people?

   Act out a scene from the attacker's past that you think might give some clue as to his behaviour or psychological state.

Sonia   *Page 30*

Isabel   *Page 31*

1 Consider the character of Sonia. What do you think she should do about her discovery? Act out the scene between her and her parents when they get home. How does she behave towards them? What does she say? What do you think their reasons are for not telling her about her adoption?

2 Consider Isabel. What do you think about her decision to have Sonia adopted? Do you agree with her when she says 'it seems best to forget'?

   Try acting out the scene where Isabel hands over her baby to the adoption officer. Do you think she'd have found it easy to let Sonia go?

3 Develop a piece of drama between Sonia and Isabel. Sonia has decided to find her real mother and arrives at Isabel's house. Before you begin, think about the following points: Does Jeff know about his wife's daughter? What is Sonia's attitude towards Isabel before meeting her? Is Jamie there when they meet? Do Sonia's adopted mum and dad know she's there?

   After the scene discuss whether you think Sonia's meeting with Isabel has helped her situation. Will they meet again?

Henry   *Page 32*

1 Read through the monologue and ask a member of the group to role play 'Henry'. Perhaps this could be teacher-in-role. The rest of the group are in role as advisers. Henry has come to you for help. By a process of hot seating, try and find out his feelings and fears and see if you can agree upon what he should do.

2 From this hot-seat activity, set up scenes where Henry puts the advice into practice. To do so you might need to discuss what his family is like and what their reaction to his news might be. After the scenes, consider whether the advice has helped Henry.

3 Other scenes to act out:
   a) Jackson telling Henry he's losing his job.
   b) Henry in the public library, bumping into someone he knows – e.g. a family friend, his daughter, etc. How can he explain his reason for being there without revealing the truth?
   c) Richard or Hilary asking their father to let them go on the school skiing trip.
   d) Henry and his wife meeting Jackson at a dinner party a few weeks after Henry's redundancy.

Paul   *Page 34*

Joan   *Page 35*

1 Consider Paul's situation. What do you think he should do? Set

up the following situations:
a) Paul telling his mother about his decision to go away to Manchester with Steve.
b) Paul staying at home and looking after his mother. (Perhaps he has just received a letter from Steve telling him about life in Manchester.)
When you have acted through these scenes, decide which decision you would make if you were in Paul's position.

2 Other scenes to act out:
a) A day in the life of Joan, living on her own.
b) One of Steve's visits to the house.
c) Paul and Steve meeting the day before Steve goes away. Will Paul be going with him?

3 *For discussion*
Paul says he'd like his mum to know about his relationship with Steve but 'it's hard to decide how she'd take it'. Discuss what you think would happen if he did tell her. Do you think he should tell her? What are the advantages and disadvantages of being 'open' about the relationship?

4 Write a monologue for Steve, showing what you see to be his attitudes, feelings and aspirations.

Stephanie	*Page 36*
Nicholas	*Page 38*
Moira	*Page 40*

1 Read through the three monologues in turn, considering the following points for each one: what is each character's over-riding priority, attitude and pattern of behaviour (e.g. secretive, outgoing, moody, etc.)?

You might like to hot seat the characters if you feel you need to know more of their background, in preparation for the role play exercise.

2 *Role play*
After using the monologues to establish the characters, set up a situation centred around the day Moira moves into the house. (Act out any preliminary scenes you feel appropriate, e.g. Stephanie and Nicholas the night before Moira arrives, Moira telling her parents she's leaving.) What problems does her arrival cause? Develop further scenes showing whether or not you think Nicholas and Moira's relationship succeeds.

Afterwards, you might choose to hot seat the characters again to find out whether the 'experience' has changed their attitudes or behaviour.

3 *Whole group improvisation game*
Each member of the group chooses a 'character' to role play. It is the first night of a new 'Companions' singles club. Each character has a specific reason for going to the club (e.g. recently divorced, new to the town, lonely, etc.) By meeting and talking with each other, try and establish who the characters are and decide which one you would like to be your 'companion'. What are you going to do to 'get off' with the person of your choice?

N.B. This is essentially a 'chatting up' game, so don't be afraid to go 'over the top'.

Kevin   *Page 41*

Janine   *Page 43*

1 Write or devise monologues for both Kevin's and Janine's fathers. What differences and/or similarities are there in their attitudes?
2 Try acting out one of the following scenes:
    a) Janine and Kevin announcing their engagement to Kevin's parents.
    b) The two families meeting each other at Janine's home. Think about the reason for Kevin's parents being invited. How do you think the situation will develop?
3 Kevin mentions that Janine is writing a book, which she is very secretive about. What do you think the book is about? Write an extract from the book which you think shows Janine's thoughts.

From this you could develop a scene where Kevin reads the extract against Janine's wishes. What might happen if she finds out he's read it?

Barry   *Page 44*

1 *For discussion*
What does the monologue reveal about our relationship with animals?

What advice would you give to anyone who visits zoos?
2 *An activity*
Make a list of three or four places you would like to go to on school visits. Give details of their attractions and links with your

school work.

Take a vote as a whole class on the most popular. You might need to consider costs and practical arrangements in planning such visits.

3 *Role work*
Try to consider circumstances in which humans would be displayed behind bars in a public place. This might be set back in time or for a particular reason. With volunteers taking their roles behind the bars set up a few moments in action.

4 *Reflection*
At the end of this role play talk about what it felt like to be behind bars.

5 To find out more about our relationship with animals invite those who work with them into school to speak to you. RSPCA workers, vets, animal trainers and those involved in animal rights might be the kind of people you would want to invite.

Lyn   *Page 45*

1 *For discussion*
How do you feel about the remark made by Lyn's mother 'Would all you men come and stand around for hours and make teas if we had an all women's team?'

Why is it that there are so few women's cricket or football teams?

Do you believe men and women are equal? Do you believe we *treat* them as equals?

2 *Pair work*
Try a few of these scenes:
The scene Lyn describes in her monologue.
– Lyn's dad and mum in confrontation after the purchase of the cricket bat.
– Lyn and her mum talking about cricket.
– Lyn and her dad in times past watching the cricket.

3 Create your own commentary of a few moments of a cricket match. You can make this very serious or use it to emphasise how sexist cricket can be.

As an extension of this, add a mime to your commentary. Remember the slow action replays can highlight key moments in your drama.

1 Between them, Sally and her mother Jill seem to have a lot of
   information about the old woman, Emily. To what extent do you
   believe this information?
        Select two members of the group to role play Sally and Jill. By a
   process of hot-seating try and find out where they get their 'facts'
   from.
2 In small groups act out some of the following scenes:
   a) Sally and a couple of friends climbing into Emily's back garden.
      What do you find? Does Emily discover them?
   b) Jill raising the matter of Emily's untidy house at a Residents
      Council meeting. Jill feels the house is 'letting down' the street's
      image. What if anything does the meeting decide to do?
   c) Emily receiving a surprise visit from one of her sons, who wants
      to persuade her to sell the house.
3 At the end of her monologue Emily says that she is afraid of going
   out for fear of being attacked. Do you think this fear is justified?
        In pairs, act out a scene between Emily and a friend – old or
   new – who can advise her what to do about her situation.

1 _Try this game_
   Sit round in a circle. The teacher calls out a series of random
   numbers in chronological order: '1,3,4,6,' etc.
        S/he pauses after each number and asks a member of the class
   to create a simple sentence about Shirley's life which relates to her
   age suggested by the number. For example:
   – 'At 1 Shirley had her first birthday party.'
   – 'When Shirley was 3 she had temper tantrums.'
   – 'At 4 she went to playgroup.'
   Continue round the circle until you reach Shirley's present age of
   40.

2 *Group work*
   Using a series of still images depict key moments in Shirley's life.
   You might need to include Terry and Val in your scenes and to
   base the ideas on both the information given in the game and on
   the details of the monologues.
3 Divide the class into three groups. Each of the groups has the task
   of giving advice to either Val, Terry or Shirley.
      Discuss the advice you might give and with three volunteers
   taking the three roles present your advice.
      The role players have the final task of responding to the advice.
4 *A final thought*
   With the advice given, how do you now see the future for Terry
   and Shirley? You can discuss the possible outcomes or devise your
   own scenes to show your ideas.

1 *For discussion*
   How was it that Angela managed to leave school without learning
   to read and write?
      Who is responsible for the problems which Angela faces?
      How would you describe the attitude of her parents?
      Read Roger's monologue carefully. If he is to become a better
   teacher, what advice would you give him?
      How could the school's organisation have helped him in his
   relationship with Angela?
2 *Solo work*
   We do not have a first-hand account from Angela in this group
   of monologues and in order to build more details about her, your
   help is invited. Find a space by yourself and think about the kind
   of girl Angela might have been when she was in Roger's class. Give
   her a personality, think about her appearance, how might she be
   dressed? Try to imagine as many details as you can.
      When you have had a few moments to think, share your ideas
   with the rest of the class. How many of your ideas were similar?

3 *Group work*
   Working in groups of three you have the task of teaching Angela
   to read and write. Remember that Angela is seventeen years
   old.

When you have decided how to approach the task, put the plan into action with one person doing the teaching, another in role as Angela and a third observing. At the end of this session the observer reports back on what s/he has seen. You might need to repeat the session putting into practice any changes you feel are appropriate and perhaps changing roles within the group.

Tanya
Page 57

1 Tanya has been taken into care at the request of her parents. Discuss what you think her history is, the incidents from her past that influenced her parents' decision, and her parents' feelings about what has happened. Consider also what you think Tanya's attitude to her mum and dad might be.
2 Try acting out some of the following scenes:
   a) Tanya's parents visiting Tanya.
   b) One of Tanya's early meetings with Rita.
   c) Mrs Freeman talking to Tanya about the girl's future.
   c) A group of kids at the home alone together in the recreation room.
3 Write a monologue for the character of Rita, showing what she thinks about the way she has treated Tanya. Are there any reasons for her behaviour?
   From this there may be other scenes you can act out telling more about what happened and why.

Bob
Page 58

1 *Pair work*
   Bob describes the scene where reporters visit him to ask questions about the toxic chemicals. Put this scene into a drama form taking the roles of the reporter and Bob.
2 *Whole class improvisation*
   An inquiry takes place at the town hall regarding the incident. Decide who will give evidence, who will pass judgment and what the outcome of the inquiry might be. You will need to set up the room you are in to represent the setting for this scene.
3 Begin your own research into pollution of seas, rivers, streams and ponds. Contact your local council to find out if any form of licensed dumping of waste is allowed. What kind of conservation groups are at work in your area?

4 Design your own poster to make people aware of the dangers of dumping toxic waste.

Samita   *Page 60*

1 *Pair work*
   Act out the scene where Samita visits Jane's mother. You will need to refer to the monologue to check the details on which to base your scene.
2 Set up a whole class still image. Imagine you are one of Jane's classmates in a social area in the school break-time. Ask a volunteer to represent Jane, or mark her presence by a chair or item of clothing. One by one take up a still position within the scene. The position you take might show how you feel about Jane
   Extend this further by speaking your thoughts towards Jane, going round the class one at a time.
3 *For Discussion*
   Do 'nicknames' hurt?
   Are Jane's classmates responsible for what happens?
   Can you remember a time when you felt hurt and humiliated in school?
   Why is it we only learn of Jane's actual name right at the end of the monologue?
4 *Research*
   Anorexia is quite a common illness amongst young people. Try to research its causes and effects. How can it be avoided?

Digga   *Page 61*

1 Consider the tone and attitude of Digga's speech. What adjectives would you use to describe him? Do you feel he is offering an honest service to pupils at the school?
2 Act out some of the following scenes:
   a) A pupil turning down Digga's 'offer' of protection.
   b) A teacher catching two members of the Protection Society trying to cram seventy-five pairs of swimming trunks into a school locker.
   c) 'A Day in the Life of Digga', ten years from now. What kind of job do you think he'll be doing? Will he have changed or developed in any way?

3 *Group Improvisation*
As a whole group, set up a street of shops. Most of them should be small family businesses, trading in a variety of goods and not directly in competition with each other. Word has gone round that a protection racket gang is planning to move in on the street. Other streets nearby have already been visited. What can the street do to protect themselves from the racketeers?

The situation can be developed by bringing other group members in in different roles, e.g. the racket gang, police officers, perhaps a local reporter who has heard about the situation.

You might also choose to use still pictures and smaller group–observed scenes to develop ideas and themes.

Nigel   *Page 62*

1 Why do you think Nigel is eager for our understanding? How well do you feel he has coped with the situation? Are his actions justified?

2 Try to describe, in writing or acting out, the most frightening moment of your life. Why were you afraid and how did you cope with it?

3 *Role play*
Act out the following situation:
Someone has locked him/herself in their house and won't come out. The person suffers from agoraphobia – a fear of open spaces. It is now two weeks since s/he dared leave the house. By developing scenes with friends, family and any 'experts' you feel might be of help, see if you can establish the cause of this person's fear and find ways of overcoming the problem.

Other phobias can be used as starting points to explore the nature of irrational fear, e.g. claustraphobia, fear of heights, water, spiders, etc.

4 *Activity*
In small groups, see if you can come up with a design for the ultimate fairground thrill machine? What are the factors that go to make up good thrill machines? You may want to give accompanying notes to explain how the machine would work in practice.

5 *Debating point*
Organise a group debate around the following statement:
'All life is sacred. Fear is no excuse for killing.' Do you agree or disagree? Present arguments for and against.

Patricia	*Page 64*
Margaret	*Page 65*
Gina	*Page 66*
Dr Ryder	*Page 67*
Rebecca	*Page 68*

1   These five monologues relate to Gina's story. Not all the information about the central incident is given. Try to find out more detail by hot-seating the characters and building up information. Are there any contradictions in what the characters tell you? If so, why do you think this happens?

2   Try 're-enacting' some of these scenes referred to in the monologues:
   a) Gina in class with Patricia and 'friends'.
   b) Rebecca's first discussion with Gina.
   c) Dr Ryder trying to get Gina to tell her story.
   d) Margaret trying to persuade Gina to come out of her room.

3   From the above activities, consider the following questions:
   a) Do you feel that Gina has coped well with the situation? How else could she have handled the problem?
   b) Do you agree with Dr Ryder's statement, 'She is not capable of leading a normal stable life and must be protected from herself'? What do you see as Gina's future?
   c) What impressions have you formed of Rebecca? What would you have done in her position?
   d) What, if anything, is the difference between justice and revenge?
   e) Is Patricia's behaviour in any way responsible for what happened?

4   *Dance drama*
   It is said that Gina lives very much in her own world. Develop a piece of dance drama capturing the thoughts and fears you think she has. To do this you need to select a piece of music which you feel captures the tone and atmosphere you want to create. 'Funeral For a Friend' by Elton John (from *Goodbye Yellow Brick Road*) could be a possible track to use. In your dance drama concentrate on capturing ideas through movement. The story you tell may have clear characters in it, alternatively you could try creating Gina's dream/nightmare through more abstract images.

5   *Role play*
   Create a 'case study' meeting about Gina, with social worker, police officer, Dr Ryder and any other people you feel necessary present. You have received reports from various sources about the

case. What do you decide to do about Gina, and how do you make that decision?

6   Other ideas that can be developed from these monologues include:

a) *Perspectives.* Create a piece of drama telling a story from different viewpoints, with each character having a different view of the 'facts'. Is it always possible to get a clear picture of things that happen?

b) *Pairs.* A young girl runs away and tracks down her real father/mother. How is she received? What are the implications for the long-lost parent?

c) *Revenge fantasy.* A person who is being constantly bullied one day discovers a secret strength-enhancing potion. After drinking it the person has superhuman powers. Should these powers be used as a chance to 'get back' at the bullies? Is there any other way of dealing with them?

British Library Cataloguing in Publication Data

Goodwin, John, *1944–*
    Solo II: further monologues for drama.
    1.Secondary schools, Curriculum subjects:
    Drama. Projects — For teaching
    I. Title   II. Taylor, Bill, *1957–*
    792′07′12

ISBN 0 340 49339 9

First published 1989
Impression number 10 9 8 7 6 5 4 3
Year   1998 1997 1996 1995 1994 1993

Typeset by Gecko Ltd, Bicester, Oxon.
Printed in Great Britain for the educational publishing division of Hodder and Stoughton Ltd, Mill Road, Dunton Green, Sevenoaks, Kent TN13 2YA by Athenæum Press Ltd, Newcastle upon Tyne.